William Blake's

# SONGS OF INNOCENCE
# AND OF EXPERIENCE

William Blake's

# SONGS OF INNOCENCE AND OF EXPERIENCE

## A STUDENT'S GUIDE

BRENDAN COOPER

PETER LANG

Oxford • Bern • Berlin • Bruxelles • Frankfurt am Main • New York • Wien

Bibliographic information published by Die Deutsche Nationalbibliothek.
Die Deutsche Nationalbibliothek lists this publication in the Deutsche
Nationalbibliografie; detailed bibliographic data is available on the Internet at
http://dnb.d-nb.de.

A catalogue record for this book is available from the British Library.

Library of Congress Control Number: 2017941148

Cover image: "The Angel" (Bentley Copy F, Plate 40) and "Holy Thursday"
(Bentley Copy F, Plate 38), Yale Center for British Art, Paul Mellon Collection.

Cover design: Peter Lang Ltd.

ISBN 978-1-78707-220-6 (print)  •  ISBN 978-1-78707-757-7 (ePDF)
ISBN 978-1-78707-758-4 (ePub)  •  ISBN 978-1-78707-759-1 (mobi)

© Peter Lang AG 2017

Published by Peter Lang Ltd, International Academic Publishers,
52 St Giles, Oxford, OX1 3LU, United Kingdom
oxford@peterlang.com, www.peterlang.com

This publication has been peer reviewed.

# Contents

# Acknowledgements

I would like to begin by thanking James O'Brien, poet, sage, and friend, for his wisdom and guidance in early stages of this project, and his invaluable input on the manuscript.

I am very grateful to Christabel Scaife and Emma Clarke at Peter Lang for their help and support in shepherding this study towards publication. I would also like to thank the Yale Center for British Art for providing the images used here.

All inspiration endlessly flows from my two daughters, Manon and Hermione.

This book is for Nouska, my light in the dark, my joy with silken twine.

# Figures

# Chronology

| | |
|---|---|
| 1803 | Blake accused of sedition by John Scofield, a soldier he had turned out of his garden. Acquitted in January 1804. |
| 1809 | Holds exhibition of his work at 28 Broad Street. Pilloried by Robert Hunt in *The Examiner*. |
| 1810 | Completes *Vala, or The Four Zoas*. |
| 1818 | Prints final version of *Milton*. |
| 1820 | First copies of *Jerusalem* printed. |
| 1821 | Moves to 3 Fountain Court, the Strand. |
| 1827 | Dies at Fountain Court, 12 August. |
| 1831 | Catherine Blake dies, 18 October. |

# 1   Introduction

> Many students of literature or painting must have
> felt that Blake's relation to those arts is a somewhat
> quizzical one. Critics in both fields insist almost
> exclusively upon the angularity of his genius.
> Blake, they tell us, is a mystic enraptured with
> incommunicable visions, standing apart, a lonely and
> isolated figure, out of touch with his own age and
> without influence on the following one.
> He is an interruption in cultural history,
> a separable phenomenon.
> (Frye 3)

So complains Northrop Frye in his monumental 1947 study of Blake, *Fearful Symmetry*. His concern was that Blake had been decontextualised – distorted by critics into a kind of mad genius, whose output cannot profitably be inserted into any larger narrative of literary, cultural, and artistic ideas. Such a view, though, remains a widespread, and in some ways under-standable response. The *Songs of Innocence and of Experience*, which remain Blake's best-known and most widely studied work, are often seen as a curiosity, offering a reading experience significantly distinct from anything else in the canon of English literature. A common initial response, on the part of readers, is a combination of dissatisfaction and puzzlement. These poems, at first glance, can seem astonishingly simple, even childish – certainly not, in any obvious way, rich enough with the kind of complexity required of serious or "great" literature.

But the *Songs*, so simple on the surface, are laden with mysteries that seem to deepen with every reading. What might have at first looked like straightforward texts become – on closer inspection – riddled with subtleties, difficulties, befuddling contradictions. Reading across the full land-scape of both "innocence" and "experience", particular words become slippery, seeming to change meaning trickily from poem to poem. The more time one spends with Blake's appar-ently accessible edifice of just over fifty short lyrics, the more it resembles a charged, tangled labyrinth of conflicting signs, buzzing with multi-layered meanings.

Few writers have managed to combine apparent simplic-ity with a reality of depthlessness like Blake did in his *Songs*. Part of the challenge – and pleasure – of reading Blake is the constant discovery of new shades of interpretation, so that these poems start to resemble the library of Borges' famous tale, "The Library of Babel", an inexhaustible space in which meaning endlessly unravels. If this is so, some crucial ques-tions emerge about how we should most profitably, most appropriately, approach the work. *How*, exactly, should we read Blake? What is the right way – if there is a right way – of accommodating ourselves to these *Songs*? How can we decode them, garner meaning from them, whilst giving adequate respect to the ways in which they seem to resist decoding?

One key challenge is their dual nature as both texts and visual images. It has become widespread, in many verse anthol-ogies and editions of Blake, for his poems to be published simply as text, without the accompanying images and designs that Blake originally produced. This process of amputating text from image – whilst undeniably convenient – inescapably distorts Blake's original creations. His plates, in their original form, demand to be interpreted as an amalgam of word and image, often with the result that a clear-cut interpretation of each plate becomes impossible. In the case of some *Songs*, the surrounding designs essentially illuminate the poems, with images depicting key figures or themes, and decorative flourishes corresponding to the poem's overall tone. For other

*Songs*, however – such as "The Little Girl Found", "Nurse's Song" from *Experience*, or "The Tyger" – there appears to be a much greater discrepancy between words and images, with the latter seeming to conflict with or ironically comment on the text, so that the plate as a whole becomes stubbornly irreducible to any single coherent framework of understanding.

Another complicating factor is the overarching structure Blake has chosen to deploy. The poems of *Innocence* were published in 1789; those of *Experience* appeared five years later. It was not until later in 1794 that Blake first published the two collections together. This initial separateness between the two volumes raises the question of how valid any holistic reading can be, that examines correspondences between the poems of "innocence" and "experience" as if they are straightforwardly part of the same project. According to Robert Essick, "we can approach *Innocence* as an autonomous work independent of direct interplay with *Experience*". At the same time, though, Essick is careful to note that "the world of *Experience* slumbers within some of the earlier songs" (Essick 9). These two collections "Shewing the two Contrary States of the Human Soul" seem, in other words, to hover in a murky no-man's-land between artistic separateness and oneness with each other. The ensuing question of precisely how the worlds of "innocence" and "experience" should be related is, as a result, both crucially important and tremendously difficult to resolve. The difficulty is not eased by the fact that Blake tended, as he produced each edition, to shift certain songs back and forth between the two collections. On top of this, even *within* each collection, different songs seem to offer conflicting perspectives on the moral, political, and spiritual ideas Blake confronts. Recognising this *dramatic* quality of the *Songs* – whereby the voices speaking each poem collectively make up a discordant choir, delivering

3

a contradictory assortment of attitudes – is fundamental to any sensitive understanding of Blake's intent.

Challenges to a comfortable interpretation of Blake even present themselves in the very methods he used to produce and publish his work. For the *Songs*, each poem and its accompanying images were drawn in reverse with acid-resistant ink onto an individual copper plate, before being dipped in acid, inked, and printed. This method gave Blake the freedom to play around with the sequencing of his songs; Blake varied the order of songs greatly throughout his life, and although the final seven copies he produced were ordered in the same way, no two surviving copies of the *Songs of Innocence and of Experience* present the poems in the same order. As a result, it becomes impossible to talk in absolute terms about a developing narrative over the course of each collection. There *is* no single narrative sequence to the *Songs* – instead, there is a whole multitude of narrative sequences, and the one any reader follows depends on which particular copy of the *Songs* they happen to be reading. Even the method of hand-painting each plate after printing, which Blake employed with the help of his wife Catherine, serves to block off any conclusive interpretation. As a result of this technique, every plate is unique, and discrepancies between different editions are, inevitably, abundant: different colours are used for the same bits of background sky; faces are sometimes masked, sometimes facing the reader; background forms are sometimes blurred, sometimes made distinct. At every level, Blake's artistic methods seem designed to resist reduction to any secure level of analytical clarity.

This is, of course, not to say that any attempt to interpret Blake's *Songs* is futile. It is simply that the right way to read Blake must be one that is sensitive to the slipperiness of his art. It is when we start to *simplify* Blake's work – to impose false coherences on his art – that we start to misread him. The *Songs* offer the reader an immensely rich and rewarding experience, but as Morris Eaves has written, "those seeking answers should keep their distance" (Eaves, "Introduction", 13).

# SONGS

## of

# INNOCENCE

## and Of

# EXPERIENCE

Shewing the Two Contrary States
of the Human Soul

# 2   What Are the *Songs* About?

The frontispiece to the *Songs* announces them as "Songs of Innocence and of Experience, Shewing the Two Contrary States of the Human Soul". The opening clues to unlocking the *Songs* lie here, within this opening plate. The reference to "the Human Soul" immediately gives an indication of Blake's project: it is, fundamentally, a spiritual one. Above all, these poems present themselves as reflections on – and expressions of – a complex series of what we might broadly call "religious" ideas. The religious dimension of the *Songs* is underlined by the image on the frontispiece, which depicts a male and female form, clearly intended to evoke Adam and Eve. The two figures are shielding themselves from surrounding tongues of flame; these flames, together with the leaves around the waists of the figures, appear to suggest their fallen state and their expulsion from Eden. Above them, by the text of the title, flies a bird commonly perceived to represent the spiritual purity – and world of innocence – from which they have now departed. This plate seems, in other words, to introduce the *Songs* as dealing with humanity's fallen-ness, inviting an interpretation of "Innocence" and "Experience" as respectively referring to pre- and post-lapsarian states.

The very same plate, though, warns against any comfortable interpretation of these poems in terms of traditional Christian theology. Here, "Innocence" and "Experience" are "Contrary States" – valid and real components of humanity, different states of mind existing simultaneously alongside each other, rather than labels used to describe man's original and fallen condition. This concept of "contraries" is central to Blake's own, highly individualistic spiritual beliefs, as well as being a core structural and artistic principle behind his composition of the *Songs*. Any reading of them must therefore keep in mind this dialectical quality to the poems – each idea, perspective, or point of view in *Innocence* will have its contrary (or various contraries) in *Experience*, and vice versa. It is not Blake's intention to resolve these conflicts, but to present them alongside one another in order to hint at a deeper, all-encompassing truth. As Peter Ackroyd, author of an influential biography of Blake, has put it, his poetry "does not unite contraries but allows them to exist in harmony beside each other" (Ackroyd 144).

Sometime between 1790 and 1793, Blake published *The Marriage of Heaven and Hell*. This is a key text in relation to the *Songs*, appearing between the two originally separate publications of *Innocence* (1789) and *Experience* (1794). *The Marriage* is written in a very different style – a strange mixture of poetry and various genres of prose, spoken in a variety of different voices – but it covers much of the same conceptual ground as the *Songs*, and helps to elucidate some of Blake's key ideas at around this time. In it, Blake writes that "Without Contraries is no progression. Attraction and Repulsion, Reason and Energy, Love and Hate, are necessary to Human existence". Blake saw the effort to separate good and evil, central to traditional Christian beliefs, as a warped effort to segregate natural components of the dynamic energy of human beings; he was always notably hostile towards the Anglican Church and its hierarchy of authority. Any understanding of the spiritual reality of mankind can, in Blake's view, only be accessed through the recognition that these contraries are constantly engaged in an antagonistic relationship within us: "Opposition is true friendship", as he states in *The Marriage*. While the traditional Christian concept of humanity's Fall is a key reference point and influential presence within the *Songs*, these poems also represent a challenge to traditional Christian perceptions of man's fallen-ness, and an effort to reconfigure a sense of spiritual truth in very different terms.

Religious ideas are therefore crucial to the *Songs*, though it would be a distortion to make any oversimplified claims that they are purely "about" religion or religious ideas. Morris Eaves has noted the many different dimensions to Blake's overall project, commenting that the *Songs* are "components in an evolving narrative of fall and redemption that is applicable on several interpenetrating levels – individual, social, religious, political, artistic, cosmic." The poems making up the *Songs* might best be understood as a complex tapestry into which these various distinct but overlapping strands of investigation are weaved. Any effort at decoding precisely what the *Songs* are *about* therefore runs up against the difficulty of disentangling these intricately intermingled aspects. One way, though, of helping to shed light on the multi-dimensional meanings of "innocence" and "experience" is through an examination of the various cultural pressures initially influencing Blake's composition of the poems.

One of the major influences on the *Songs* – and one which helps to account for the apparent simplicity of Blake's language – was the ballad and hymn literature for children that was popular throughout the eighteenth century. In 1715, Isaac Watts – whose hymns remained in print throughout the century – published *Divine Songs for Children*. In this collection, Watts displays a clear desire to educate children about the realities of poverty and social inequality:

> Whene'er I take my walks abroad,
> How many poor I see!
> What shall I render to my God,
> For all his gifts to me
>
> Not more than others I deserve,
> Yet God hath given me more;
> For I have food, while others starve,
> Or beg from door to door.

> How many children in the street
> Half-naked I behold!
> While I am clothed from head to feet,
> And covered from the cold.

The setting Watts presents here – of the speaker walking through the dismal streets of a city, and commenting upon the scenes of suffering they encounter – anticipates Blake's "London". Watts' influence can also be traced in Blake's "Chimney Sweeper" poems, though Blake replaces Watts' simplistic moralising with a much more complex picture of the children he describes. John Beer has even suggested that some of Blake's Songs read like "satirical versions of, or answers to" Watts' verses (Beer 7).

In Blake's own lifetime, Christopher Smart published *Hymns for the Amusement of Children* (1771). In "Mirth" from this collection, a celebration of childhood freedom and merriment is described that anticipates Blake's presentation of children in the *Songs*:

> If you are merry sing away,
> And touch the organs sweet;
> This is the Lord's triumphant day,
> Ye children in the gall'ries gay
> Shout from each goodly seat.
>
> It shall be May to-morrow's morn,
> Afield then let us run,
> And deck us in the blooming thorn,
> Soon as the cock begins to warn,
> And long before the sun.

It is ultimately imprecise simply to state that innocence symbolises childhood in the *Songs*, with experience symbolising adulthood. There is clearly, though, an overall pattern throughout the two collections of a progression towards adulthood involving a shift from innocence to experience. One key thing that the *Songs* are "about" is the fluctuating levels of innocence and experience within us in the course of our inevitable journey out of childhood into the adult world. Blake does not present this simply as a negative development: in "The Shepherd" and the "Nurse's Song" of *Innocence*, for example, adult figures offer a sense of protective support, representing (amongst other things) dependability and wisdom. More commonly, though, Blake presents the authority of the adult presence as a damaging restriction of the spiritual purity and natural human vibrancy of children. Ackroyd identifies a "continual threat of parental tyranny" in Blake's poetry – perhaps based, he argues, on an ambivalent relationship between Blake and his own parents (Ackroyd 8). A mistrust of parental figures – particularly fathers – is certainly evident in numerous Songs, such as "The Little Boy Lost", where the father appears to abandon his son ("The night was dark, no father was there"), only to be replaced by the divine Father in "The Little Boy Found" ("… God ever nigh/Appeared like his father in white"). The point is further enforced by Blake's illustration, in which the "Father" figure is depicted as a feminised fusion of a mother and Jesus.

Blake lived and wrote in notably volatile times. It was an era of sweeping industrial and political change, set to an international backdrop of revolutions in both America and France: the *Songs of Innocence* were themselves published in 1789, the year of the French Revolution. It is perhaps unsurprising, in the light of this, that Blake's Songs are richly political poems, in various senses of the term – commenting on the social conditions surrounding him in late eighteenth-century London, and often directly attacking the authority of state institutions. Many of the Songs – "London", the "Chimney Sweeper" poems, and "Holy Thursday", for instance – highlight the awful conditions of the poor and express anger at economic inequality and social injustice. These same poems, together with various others (such as "The Garden of Love", "The Little Vagabond", and "A Little Boy Lost") attack the hypocrisy and oppression Blake saw in the Church, underlining the deeply dissenting, anti-traditional nature of his own religious vision. Blake was highly sympathetic to the ideas of Thomas Paine, whose pamphlet *Common Sense*, supporting American independence, was published in 1776; Paine's *Rights of Man* appeared in 1791–2, exerting an influence upon Blake's poems of *Experience*. The radical and subversive politics of the *Rights of Man* led to Paine being tried and found guilty of seditious libel in 1792, whilst he was in France. Blake's poems are, in other words, very much "about" the volatile late eighteenth-century cultural context in which he wrote, with many Songs containing a directly political dimension that sits alongside his multiple other engagements.

The only adequately sensitive conclusion to be drawn from this is that the *Songs* deal in complicated ways with a wide array of spiritual, political, and philosophical ideas in a manner that is too intricate to be easily reduced to straightforward thematic analysis. Ultimately, though – if anything can be said to reside at the heart of these challenging and mysterious poems – it is the religious vision that Blake is so passionately seeking to communicate. It has been said of Blake that nothing can be found in his work that cannot first be found in the Bible – an inevitable exaggeration that nevertheless underlines how saturated his poetry is with innumerable Biblical images, references, and motifs, all incorporated into his own highly personalised, anti-authoritarian religious stance. Blake's eighteenth-century audience will have been far more familiar with these than the majority of contemporary readers, and it is all too easy for a reader who lacks extensive Biblical knowledge to underestimate the presence of the Bible in the *Songs*.

Whilst these poems are nothing if not "religious", though, the nature of Blake's artistic methods makes it difficult to understand them in terms of a coherent set of theological ideas. Blake's mistrust of rationalism is one of the defining features of his life and work, setting him apart from Enlightenment thinkers such as Voltaire and David Hume, and making him steadfastly opposed to argumentatively consistent dogma. The dramatic framework of the *Songs* means that in each poem we might encounter a particular view that is contradicted elsewhere; as Robert Ryan has said, "different dramatic voices express conflicting theological views", so that "his verses can be quoted convincingly on both sides of any important religious question" (Ryan, "Blake and Religion", 165). Blake's *Songs* are undeniably "religious" poems, but it is equally undeniable that the religiosity they display is of a very unusual and mysterious kind.

SONGS

Innocence

1789

The Author & Printer W Blake

# 3 The Meaning of "Innocence" in the *Songs*

A variety of associations hover around the word "innocence", and in the *Songs* Blake was clearly exploiting some of its ambiguities. At one level, "innocence" has resonances which are specific to particular theological ideas and religious traditions; at the same time, the word also has resonances which are more everyday, stemming from the word's common English usage. There is little doubt that Blake intended his readers to make associations between the world of innocence he depicts and humanity's original Edenic innocence as outlined in the Book of Genesis. It is equally clear, though, that Blake had no intention of confining his concept of innocence, and the poems he groups under it, to such a specifically religious dimension. Blake does, for instance, see "innocence" not as a lost origin so much as a component of humanity discoverable, in particular, in the unique qualities of childhood. Many of the *Songs of Innocence* either describe children, or are spoken in the voice of a child; in these poems, there is a clear association of "innocence" with the naivety, inexperience, and uncorrupted goodness of early life.

The *meaning* of "innocence" is strongly linked both to Blake's fractious engagement with the Christian idea of original innocence, and also to the notion of childhood as a time of untainted goodness and spiritual purity. But "innocence" is not a word that can so easily be categorised as positive, and in these poems Blake is alive to this complexity. The sense of purity the word connotes – of freedom from moral guilt, or corruption – lends it a positive and optimistic air; but "innocence" also connotes a lack of knowledge and understanding – a fragile naivety, as well as a lack of vibrant energy – that makes it both vulnerable and less than fully adequate. Throughout these poems, Blake develops a complex sense of the meaning of "innocence" by playing on the limitations of the state of innocence at the same time as he celebrates its qualities of freedom and purity.

In the title plate to *Innocence*, a mother or nurse is displayed showing a book to a young boy and a young girl. Here, the relationship is a harmonious one between adult and child figures, with the former appearing to offer education to the children in her care. Some of the details of the image, though, are more mysterious. The girl is pointing at something, though in some copies it looks more like she is holding something in her hand – actually writing, or drawing, upon the page. The boy beside her is staring at the book from a sideways-on position – as if regarding an image, rather than reading a text. The mother/nurse is watching them, not the book, and is not speaking – existing here as a conduit to whatever wisdom or pleasure the book offers, rather than communicating any knowledge herself. The words of the title, "SONGS of INNOCENCE", are written above them as sinuous and graceful branches, leaves, and tendrils, many of which directly flow out of a tree located in the bottom right corner. These features anticipate another key theme throughout the poems of *Innocence*, that of nature: poems like "Laughing Song", "The Ecchoing Green", and "Nurse's Song" in *Innocence* all present the green pastures of nature as a landscape within which freedom and happiness are made possible, especially (though not exclusively) to children. The overall sense in this title plate is of children contentedly educating themselves in the presence of an adult, outside in the freedom and beauty of the natural world rather than confined inside a schoolroom.

A comprehensive understanding of what Blake means by "innocence" is, given the nature of his approach, a rather elusive prospect. But a very helpful reference point in this regard is the "Introduction" to *Innocence*, which establishes some of Blake's key concerns in this collection, and sets the tone for what is to follow. In this piece, the poet is provided with artistic inspiration by a muse-like child, whose appearance "on a cloud" hints at his divine or angelic qualities. In the image accompanying the poem, which is given a plate of its own, this child-muse is drawn with curiously over-developed muscularity – perhaps to highlight that he is not human, or to emphasise his imaginative power, or even to hint that this angelic figure is not purely "innocent". This same image also helps to link this piece – and by extension, the whole sequence of *Innocence* poems – with the tradition of pastoral verse. The poet-figure is depicted as a shepherd, his flock of sheep grazing behind him. The flock appears as one vast mass – as if physically conjoined, a single organic body, suggesting the qualities of unity and harmony associated with the state of innocence throughout these poems.

To begin with, the poet here is a "piper", an artist whose medium is music rather than words. In the first line he is "Piping down the valleys wild": the pastoral theme, suggested in the image, is supported here with an apparently idyllic rural setting. The word "wild", though, suggests something harsher than the mild and cultivated natural landscapes of traditional pastoral verse. In the light of other poems, such as "The Little Girl Lost" (originally published in *Innocence*) – where the girl and ultimately her parents live among "tygers wild" – the word has connotations of sexual energy and physical danger. It even foreshadows the threatening "forests of the night" where Blake's "tyger" dwells in *Experience*. Already, then – in the very first line of the entire collection – Blake is gently complicating his portrayal of innocence, by hinting at the contrary qualities of experience with which innocence overlaps and upon which it depends.

The happily "laughing" child begins by requesting the poet to play his pipe:

Pipe a song about a lamb.
So I piped with merry chear.
Piper, pipe that song again.
So I piped: he wept to hear.

The repetition of "pipe" and its variants here emphasises the poet's musical activity and creates a merry, songlike musicality of its own. The lack of quotation marks – typical of many *Songs* – blurs the boundary between the two voices, and helps to create the effect of them overlapping, as if the child is actually a part of the poet's own self. It is significant that the song here is "about a lamb": the lamb is a symbol of innocence throughout these poems, and is also exploited for its associations with Christ. Robert Essick says of this introduction that "[a]s a shepherd and a mediator between earthbound and higher states of consciousness, the piper is also a Christ-like figure" (Essick 26); Blake creates bonds here of a spiritual nature between the angelic child-muse, the piper-poet, and the song he plays in its celebration of a lamb, or Lamb of God. Even the fine details of Blake's eccentric spelling are rich with encoded meaning. The spelling of "cheer" as "chear", with the word "hear" contained inside it, is a kind of textual embodiment of the non-verbal beauty of the poet's music – a kind of beauty that cannot itself be translated into words.

The rest of the "Introduction", whilst appearing to celebrate artistic inspiration, in fact expresses ambivalence about the progression of the piper's music into language. At the poet's conversion of the music into song, the child "wept with joy", but the child vanishes the moment he completes the request that the song be converted to written language. The reed plucked by the poet is "hollow", hinting that it is lacking in some way; it has even been suggested that "hollow reed" could be a pun on "hollow read", and that the reading of text is itself relatively impoverished compared to its original poetic inspiration. As he prepares to write, the poet "stain[s] the water clear" – an image ostensibly describing the concoction of his pigments, but which also reads as an image of contamination, as if the purity of the original music is being lost – as if, perhaps, the conversion of artistic feeling into words its itself a loss of innocence.

The "Introduction", then, with its various subtleties laced into an apparently simple, happy tale, provides an outline of some of the intricacies surrounding what "innocence" means in these poems. Innocence is a state of freedom, purity, and joy, but darker shadows tend to hover over it, indicating the fundamental interdependence of innocence and experience. The poem which best captures the spiritual optimism and harmony of innocence is "The Lamb", in which the lamb's Biblical associations with Christ are developed ("Look, the Lamb of God, who takes away the sin of the world!", John 1:29). In Blake's poem, the narrator – a shepherd-child – repeatedly asks the lamb, in the first stanza, about its creator: "Little Lamb who made thee?/Dost thou know who made thee?" In the second stanza, where these questions are answered, the child proposes a unity between the lamb, himself, and Christ as their creator: "He became a little child,/I a child and thou a lamb,/We are called by his name." Christ, as Lamb of God and as the good shepherd ("I am the good shepherd: the good shepherd giveth his life for the sheep", John 10:11), is joined in name and in spirit with the lamb and the narrator. The inclusive language of "We are called by his name" even draws the reader into an identification with Christ, so that the poem becomes a spiritual forge in which humanity, nature, and Christ are united.

Whilst it is difficult to read "The Lamb" as anything other than a joyful celebration of mankind's spiritual nature as embodied in Christ, elsewhere Blake's presentation of innocence is more complicated and ambivalent. Frequently, the children of innocence are exposed as vulnerable and in need of protection. In "The Little Girl Lost", the heroine is "Lost in desert wild", while the boy of "The Little Boy Lost" is left abandoned by his father. In "The Shepherd", the titular character "is watchful" while his flock is in peace, and the flock "know when their shepherd is nigh": the implication is that the sheep under his watch can only remain happy because he is there to guard them. The shepherd appears here once again as a Christ-like figure, but also, importantly, as an adult, a figure from experience, whose protective eye is a necessary counterpart to the peaceful, childish freedoms of the world of innocence.

In fact, throughout the *Songs of Innocence*, hints of experience persistently encroach as a sort of corrective force to the anodyne purity of innocence. Blake was no believer in the rejection of physicality, or even in the exclusive pursuit of "good", and his departure from traditional Christian morality is significant here. "Good is the passive that obeys reason. Evil is the active springing from Energy", runs one passage in *The Marriage*, before the point is made even more provocatively: "Sooner murder an infant in its cradle than nurse unacted desires." For Blake, the passivity and untaintedness of innocence were, ultimately, indications of its incompleteness and inadequacy. Its completion could only be enabled via the vibrancy, sexuality, and passion of experience. In "Spring", even the figure of the lamb becomes playfully linked with images of sensuality and physical desire:

> Little lamb
> Here I am.
> Come and lick
> My white neck.
> Let me pull
> Your soft wool.
> Let me kiss
> Your soft face,
> Merrily, merrily we welcome in the year.

The atmosphere here is happy and light, but the sexual undertones are obvious enough to exist as a complicating factor, injecting a provocative element into a scene that at first glance might appear simply to be one of childish play. Robert Essick, while noting the effect of "baby talk" in this poem, also points out that "the speaker could be an adult speaking to a very young child or even to a pre-linguistic infant" (Essick 67): the scene may appear to describe innocence, but the perspective from which it is described is not necessarily innocent at all. Innocence, then, not only *requires* its contrary state, but rarely appears without some indication of its presence. Blake's vision ultimately reveals innocence to be untenable without the darker, more corrupt, but more vibrant and animated state of experience that he was to explore in his contrary collection.

# Introduction.

Hear the voice of the Bard!
Who Present, Past, & Future sees
Whose ears have heard,
The Holy Word,
That walk'd among the ancient trees.

Calling the lapsed Soul
And weeping in the evening dew:
That might controll.
The starry pole;
And fallen fallen light renew!

O Earth O Earth return!
Arise from out the dewy grass;
Night is worn,
And the morn
Rises from the slumberous mass.

Turn away no more:
Why wilt thou turn away
The starry floor
The watry shore
Is given thee till the break of day.

# 4    The Meaning of "Experience" in the *Songs*

The question of whether Blake had already planned to write the poems of *Experience* when he wrote and published the *Songs of Innocence* remains unanswerable, a matter less for analysis than for speculation. But the scattering of darker and more troubling material throughout the peace and harmony of *Innocence* makes it clear enough that Blake had, already, fully recognised not just the limitations of innocence as a state but also its incompleteness. David Erdman, an influential critic on Blake, argues that "only a person aware of much amiss and seeking a cloak against ill winds could have made Blake's conscious creative effort to organise a place of shelter for Wisdom and Innocence, lion and lamb, to dwell in together"; it is "misleading", he suggests, to think that Blake had composed the *Songs of Innocence* without any clear sense of their contrary (Erdman 115). The necessary presence of experience, intertwined with innocence and both complementing and conflicting with it, is built into Blake's initial collection.

Achieving a clear overall sense of the meaning of "experience" is, once again, a slippery proposition, as Blake invests these poems with a complex array of ideas, imbuing the state of experience with an intricate combination of both positive and negative qualities. With the arrival of experience, there is undeniably a strong sense of loss; there are heavy associations throughout the *Songs of Experience* with pain, suffering, moral corruption and decay. But there is also wisdom in experience: the naivety of innocence has been replaced by knowledge. In place of the insipid purity of innocence, there is vibrant physicality and power. There is a shift from rural to more urban settings, often bleak ones; and Blake's political dimension is stronger here, with many *Songs* raging against social and political injustice. As always, Blake is not interested in dogmatically or even consistently asserting a particular position, so much as exploring a variety of intermingled ideas through his use of competing dramatic voices.

The poems of *Experience* begin with an "Introduction" that is perhaps the most ambiguous and difficult poem in the whole of the *Songs*. Here, Blake's punctuation and syntax is so befuddling that a full decoding of the piece is impossible; various, directly conflicting interpretations instead coexist alongside each other. The "piper" of innocence has now been replaced by the "Bard" – a prophetic figure "who past, present and future sees". It is not made fully clear whether this Bard is the poet himself, or another figure distinct from him. The gentleness of *Innocence* is replaced here by urgency, evident in the imperative of the opening line:

Hear the voice of the Bard!
Who present, past and future sees;
Whose ears have heard
The Holy Word,
That walked among the ancient trees

Calling the lapsed soul,
And weeping in the evening dew;
That might control
The starry pole,
And fallen, fallen light renew!

The basic sense of yearning for a retrieval of lost spiritual unity is clear enough. References to the "Holy Word", the "lapsed soul" and "fallen light" reveal Blake to be adopting the theology of the Fall, but the nature of his religious vision is highly unorthodox, and deeply enigmatic. Just who is the agent of possible redemption? The syntactical and grammatical ambiguity of these lines makes it unclear whether it is the "Bard" or "the Holy Word" who "walked among the ancient trees", and whether it is either of these – or even the "lapsed soul" – who in fact might ultimately "renew" the fallen light of the world. The reference to the Bard hearing the Holy Word may hint at Adam's hearing of the voice of God in the Garden of Eden in Genesis 3:8. The difficulty deepens in the third and fourth stanzas, when a new voice – which may or may not be the Bard himself – pleads for a return of the Earth ("O Earth, O Earth return!/Arise from out the dewy grass"). As an opening to *Experience*, this poem delivers a strong sense of despair in the face of a corrupt and broken world, but the crucial departures he makes from traditional Christian theology are written into the oddities and difficulties of the piece. As F. R. Leavis summarised, Blake's purpose here is not to deliver a coherent thesis, but to express "his own particular intuition of evil, disharmony and a general fall."

In Blake's sequencing of *Songs*, the "Introduction" was always immediately followed by "Earth's Answer", which functions as a counterpart poem and helps to clarify aspects of Blake's opaque ideas. In the reply of Earth here, there is a desperate desire expressed for freedom from suffering and oppression:

> Break this heavy chain
> That does freeze my bones around.
> Selfish! Vain!
> Eternal bane!
> That free love with bondage bound

Blake again chooses unusual images here to represent mankind's fallen state. The sense is of "free love" being painfully restricted by forces of oppression; there is a clear sense of social, political, and religious authority constraining and crushing mankind's natural freedom. Together, these introductory poems indicate both the highly personalised religious dimension of the poems of experience, as well as their more overtly political quality. The idea of a spiritual *brokenness* that

25

requires healing becomes tangled up with a current of radical political invective against the destructive and oppressive powers of governmental and religious institutions.

The poem that comes closest to defining the "meaning" of *Experience* is probably its most famous, "The Tyger". This piece exists as a counterpoint to "The Lamb", incorporating many of the key qualities of the state of experience as well as embodying some of its most noteworthy contradictions. Despite the poem's fame and omnipresence in literary anthologies of all kinds, it is a deeply challenging and mysterious work which again displays Blake's genius for embedding deep obscurities within language of apparently childlike simplicity. The whole poem is structured as a series of questions, which begin:

> Tyger Tyger burning bright
> In the forests of the night:
> What immortal hand or eye
> Could frame thy fearful symmetry?

In "The Lamb", the child who speaks the poem, the lamb itself, and Christ are melded into a perfect harmony: there is an unproblematic sense of unity between humanity, nature, and God. Here, the poet is overtly struggling to fit the "tyger" within any overarching scheme of divine purpose. The "fearful symmetry" it possesses appears to have both a moral and a physical dimension: the poet wonders how a creature representing such dynamism and physical power could ever have been "framed" by a controlling deity, at the same time as he questions the consistency of such threatening force with notions of divine goodness. And yet the tyger is not presented here in simply negative terms. It is a creature of the "night" – a time associated throughout the *Songs* with danger, threat, and suffering, for example in the "midnight streets" of "London". But within this setting, the tiger is "burning bright" – at the same time as the burning might suggest Hellish flame, the tyger is appearing as a light within the darkness, whose dynamic energy might even prefigure the renewal of "fallen light" yearned for so desperately in the "Introduction".

As a whole, "The Tyger" underlines the ambiguous nature of experience and again reinforces the dependence of innocence and experience upon each other. On one level, the tyger can be seen as embodying corruption, evil, and violence – not just at a spiritual level, but at a social and political level too. In the fourth stanza it is associated with the harsh forces of mechanical production:

> What the hammer? What the chain?
> In what furnace was thy brain?
> What the anvil? What dread grasp
> Dare its deadly terrors clasp?

There is a dark and oppressive feel here to these images of artificial rather than natural creation, and the reference to a "furnace" again conjures up a feeling of infernal malice. Even these images, though, convey a striking power and vitality that, amongst other things, evokes the material processes of Blake's own art, in which metal words have forged from burning acid (in *The Marriage of Heaven and Hell*, Blake asserts that he will print "in the infernal method, by corrosives, which in Hell are salutary and medicinal, melting apparent surfaces away, and displaying the infinite which was hid"). The effervescent energy of the poem can also be linked with revolutionary spirit that had so recently toppled the established regimes of America and France. Frightening and seductive, powerful and threatening, destructive and dynamic, the tyger is both the antithesis of "The Lamb" and its necessary counterpart, and it is the immense difficulty of synthesising these two complementary but antagonistic symbols into a single religious vision that lies behind the unanswered questions out of which the poem is composed: "Did he smile his work to see?/Did he who made the lamb make thee?"

"The Tyger" is also an excellent example of Blake's apparently simple, but highly skilful use of form. The poem is largely written in trochaic metre, with an extra, stressed syllable at the end of each line. This creates a symmetrical structure that mimics the "fearful symmetry" of the tyger itself:

> Tyger Tyger **burning bright**
> **In** the **for**ests **of** the **night:**

The seven-syllable lines, each beginning and ending with the force of a stressed syllable, have an imposing feel that fits with the power and violence of Blake's tiger. But Blake's metrical variations also serve subtly to complement nuances in the poem's meaning. The first stanza closes with the following lines:

> **What** im**mor**tal **hand** or **eye**
> Could **frame** thy **fear**ful **symmetry?**

Here, the fourth line appears as a disruption to formal regularity. Instead of full rhyme, Blake delivers the apparent "eye rhyme" of "eye" and "symmetry": whether these words actually did rhyme, to Blake's ears, has been a vexed question in critical discussions of his work, but there is evidence to suggest that they did not fully rhyme in eighteenth-century English, making the apparent disruption deliberate. In addition, the metre of line four is different – the symmetrical seven-syllable lines give way to an eight-syllable line of iambic tetrameter. These details create a hint of disharmony, signifying the conceptual struggle being described. The speaker's incredulity about the tiger being successfully "framed" by the hands of any kind of creator is, in other words, heightened by the formal disruptions Blake injects into this moment in the poem. Throughout the *Songs*, Blake's approach to form often functions in this way, with his apparently simple use of rhyme and rhythm in fact existing as a vehicle for the skilful, complex manipulation of subtleties of meaning.

The overall tenor of the poems of *Experience* is without question much darker and more troubled that that of *Innocence*. The "meaning" of experience is closely associated with a sharp sense of humanity as separated from spiritual truth and requiring redemption and renewal. Tied into this is a presentation of the Church itself as a malign force of oppression, directly hindering humanity's capacity to gain such spiritual redemption. In "London", the "black'ning church" is implicitly responsible for the suffering of the city's chimney sweepers; in "The Garden of Love", the "priests in black gowns" are "walking their rounds", "binding with briars" the poet's "joys and desires"; in "A Little Boy Lost", a priest inflicts terrifying verbal and physical abuse on the boy, burning him for daring to question the established precepts of the Church:

> The priest sat by had heard the child;
> In trembling zeal he seized his hair.
> He led him by his little coat,
> And all admired his priestly care.
>
> And standing on the altar high,
> "Lo, what a fiend is here!" said he,
> "One who sets reason up for judge
> Of our most holy mystery."

These bleak and angry lines might, on the surface, appear inconsistent with the visions of spiritual harmony and delight Blake tends to deliver in *Innocence*, but in fact they are part of the very same religious vision. Blake's belief was in humanity's intrinsically divine nature, and in our basic capacity – with liberated vision and understanding – to access this divinity. As he famously puts it in *The Marriage of Heaven & Hell*, "If the doors of perception were cleansed every thing would appear to man as it is, infinite". It is this process of cleansing, of accessing the divine within the fabric of the surrounding world and within ourselves, that is at the heart of Blake's visionary project in the *Songs*.

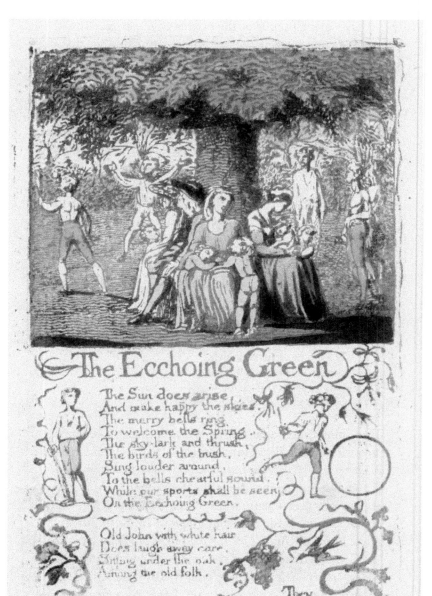

# The Ecchoing Green

The Sun does arise,
And make happy the skies;
The merry bells ring
To welcome the Spring.
The sky-lark and thrush,
The birds of the bush,
Sing louder around,
To the bells chearful sound,
While our sports shall be seen
On the Ecchoing Green.

Old John with white hair
Does laugh away care,
Sitting under the oak,
Among the old folk.

They

## 5  Nature and the Pastoral

One of the more conspicuous curiosities of Blake's poetry –
and of the *Songs* in particular – is the extent to which he
depicts and praises the beauty of nature. For Blake was a notably, almost uniquely urban poet. He left London only once,
spending almost the entirety of his life in particular environs
of the city: the Strand, Holborn, Oxford Street, Lambeth.
Blake's narrow subsistence in these parts of London hardly
suggests a passionate interest in the beauty or significance of
rural surroundings. It is somewhat surprising, then, to see
Blake invest in the pastoral tradition with such verve: in these
*Songs*, nature is imbued with rich spiritual energy, frequently
becoming the space in which individuals can discover happiness and freedom. It is, for this reason, closely intertwined
with both childhood and Blake's conception of "innocence":
nature is a kind of gateway to spirituality, the place that most
richly allows for contentment, a haven of peace outside the
grip of social, political, and religious institutions.

In "The Ecchoing Green", for instance, a child describes
a scene of frivolity and play in a landscape of natural beauty
and harmony:

> The Sun does arise,
> And make happy the skies.
> The merry bells ring
> To welcome the Spring.
> The sky-lark and thrush,
> The birds of the bush,
> Sing louder around,
> To the bells' chearful sound,
> While our sports shall be seen
> On the Ecchoing Green.

The emphasis here is on the complementary unities of nature – the sun contributes to the sky's happiness, and the birds' song is energised by the sound of the bells; the green is "ecchoing" not just with the children's play, but with the harmonious reverberations of the natural world. It is significant, in this Song, to find various generations happily gathered together. We are told that "Old John with white hair/Does laugh away care": the presence of his "care" reminds us here of the burdens of the adult world, but it is lifted by his presence on the green and his participation in youthful play. The adult nostalgia for childhood freedoms is delivered as fond and affectionate reminiscence: another "ecchoing" here is that which takes place so agreeably between generations. In the last stanza, the end of the day brings the sorts of hints at darkness that are recurrently to be found in *Innocence*. Sport is "no more seen/On the darkening green", a conclusion that could be read as a metaphor for the inevitable disappearance of youthful freedom. The "green" of this poem is a geographical space in which innocence can celebrate itself, in all its lightness, purity, and transience.

A similar portrait of joy within a rural setting is delivered in "Laughing Song":

> When the green woods laugh with the voice of joy,
> And the dimpling stream runs laughing by,
> When the air does laugh with our merry wit
> And the green hill laughs with the noise of it,
>
> When the meadows laugh with lively green
> And the grasshopper laughs in the merry scene,
> When Mary and Susan and Emily
> With their sweet round mouths sing "Ha, Ha, he!"

The intermingling of natural landscape and living presence is again significant here. The woods, the stream, the air, the hill, the meadows and the grasshopper all laugh with each other in a picture of absolute and perfect unison. The importance of greenness is also once again clear; Blake evidently wishes to emphasise it as a visual signal of nature's beauty and vitality, drawing on a tradition of colour symbolism stretching back to the folk mythology of the Green Man. Only very gently might it also hint at another of its meanings, suggesting naivety or inexperience. The reference to the "sweet round mouths" of the female figures here lends the poem an odd note of sensuality, puncturing the apparent purity of the scene. As is so often the case, Blake complicates his vision of innocence by subtly demonstrating the inescapable presence of the world of experience, upon which it must ultimately depend.

In the light of this tendency to present nature in reverential terms, it is tempting to conclude that Blake saw the relationship between the rural and the urban as essentially a conflict between freedom and oppression. It is certainly the case that city spaces tend to be spaces of suffering in the *Songs*: an urban poet Blake may be, but one of lament for its deficiencies far more than celebration of its virtues. In "The Chimney Sweeper" from *Experience*, the boy is clothed by his parents in the "clothes of death" – the distinctive rags of sweepers – "Because I was happy upon the heath,/And smil'd among the winters snow". It is specifically the child's happiness that motivates the brutality and sadism of the parents here, and it is in nature – on the "heath", in the "snow" – that he has been happily playing. Blake's accompanying illustration, depicting a grim city backstreet battered by rain, highlights the dismal urban environment to which the boy has now been condemned. Famously, in "London", Blake attacks the suffering and iniquity he encounters in the city, with the power of governmental authorities envisaged as a kind of disease infecting the very fabric of nature itself (the "charter'd Thames"). Disease is also the subject of the poem's last stanza:

> But most through midnight streets I hear
> How the youthful Harlots curse
> Blasts the newborn infants tear
> And blights with plagues the marriage hearse.

It is of note that the action takes place here in "midnight streets": the squalor and danger of the London night, together with its suggested spiritual darkness, contrasts sharply with the daylight joy of natural landscapes throughout *Innocence*. The "Harlots curse" here is, primarily, that of venereal disease – infecting not only the man who solicits the prostitute but also consequently his wife, together with their newborn baby, whose crying encapsulates the omnipresence of suffering in this environment from the very beginning of life. The fact that the harlot is "youthful" indicates that her own innocence has been poisoned. Blake's London is an infernal nightmare, an apocalypse of despair that both highlights his raging contempt for governmental and religious authority and also suggests his feelings of dejection about a city in which he continued so loyally to live and work.

Any effort, though, to interpret nature simply as a beautiful utopia, and the city simply as an abyss of horror, does not do justice to the slippery quality of Blake's portrayal of nature in the *Songs*. Nature is, often, a pastoral idyll; it is also, at times, a space of danger, threat, and sexual exploration. The gentle tension in the words "valleys wild" at the very beginning of the "Introduction" to *Innocence* – a tension between nature as cosy pastoral rusticity, and nature as menacing wilderness – embodies a dual quality to the natural world that runs throughout the entirety of Blake's work. The openness of nature brings both freedom and vulnerability, both opportunity and fear. In "The Little Girl Lost", the girl, Lyca, is lost in a form of natural environment which becomes very different to the comfortable, cultivated greens Blake describes elsewhere:

> In the southern clime,
>   Where the summer's prime
>   Never fades away,
>   Lovely Lyca lay.

Seven summers old
 Lovely Lyca told.
 She had wandered long,
 Hearing wild birds' song.

'Sweet sleep, come to me,
 Underneath this tree;
 Do father, mother, weep?
 Where can Lyca sleep?

'Lost in desert wild
 Is your little child.
 How can Lyca sleep
 If her mother weep?

The "desert wild" described here begins as the scene of Lyca's abandonment and despair, but becomes an arena of sexual discovery as she is discovered by "beasts of prey". The language is increasingly charged with eroticism, as Blake emphasises the animals' kidnapping of the girl as a metaphor of her sexual enlightenment. Lyca is described as a "maid", a "virgin"; the lion is "kingly", a figure of masculine power, provocatively licking Lyca's neck before the lioness removes her "slender dress" and they all carry her naked body to their caves. In this poem, the freedom of nature becomes a platform for a journey away from innocence, with wildness an emblem for a form of dark, dynamic natural environment more in tune with the physicality and risk of experience.

Typically, then, Blake's presentation of nature is contradictory, shifting in significant ways from poem to poem. In *Experience*, darker, more sexual meanings are more frequently injected into his descriptions of the natural world. In "The Sick Rose", the phallic "invisible worm" has found out the rose's bed of "crimson joy" (a phrase laden with undertones of deflowering), and "his dark secret love" destroys the rose's "life" – perhaps signifying the extinction of her spiritual purity, or the infliction of venereal disease. The entirety of this poem can be read as a metaphor for the taking of a virgin's innocence by a threatening, predatory male presence. Another poem, "My Pretty Rose Tree", comparably captures the presence of a darker, more harmful side to nature, with the "rose" becoming a complex symbol of both beauty and danger, seductive charm and threatening malice:

> A flower was offered to me,
> Such a flower as May never bore,
> But I said, "I've a pretty rose tree,"
> And I passed the sweet flower o'er.
>
> Then I went to my pretty rose tree,
> To tend her by day and by night,
> But my rose turned away with jealousy,
> And her thorns were my only delight.

The narrator's masochistic delight in the rose's "thorns" here indicates a dark attraction to the dangers of nature as well as metaphorically indicating the lover's revelry in his unrequited passion. The overall picture of nature in the *Songs of Innocence and of Experience* is wide-ranging, complex, and inconsistent. For all its associations with childhood and unencumbered spiritual enlightenment, nature is also unavoidably the "forests of the night" evoked in "The Tyger", a space whose untamed sublimity is both frightening and exciting. It is, like all of Blake's key concerns, a phenomenon with many faces, the complexities of which Blake steadily illuminates as he steps from song to song.

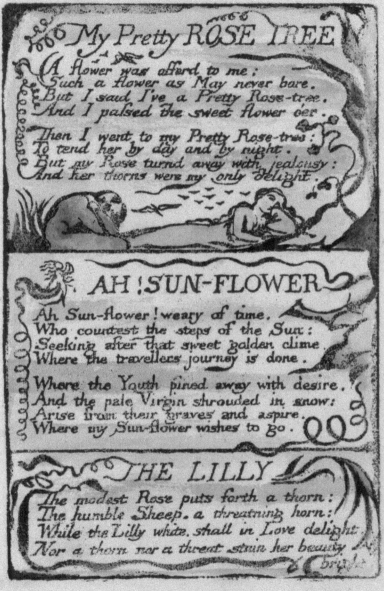

# My Pretty ROSE TREE

A flower was offerd to me:
Such a flower as May never bore.
But I said I've a Pretty Rose-tree.
And I passed the sweet flower o'er.

Then I went to my Pretty Rose-tree:
To tend her by day and by night.
But my Rose turnd away with jealousy:
And her thorns were my only delight.

# AH ! SUN-FLOWER

Ah Sun-flower ! weary of time.
Who countest the steps of the Sun:
Seeking after that sweet golden clime.
Where the travellers journey is done.

Where the Youth pined away with desire.
And the pale Virgin shrouded in snow:
Arise from their graves and aspire.
Where my Sun-flower wishes to go.

# THE LILLY

The modest Rose puts forth a thorn:
The humble Sheep. a threatning horn:
While the Lilly white. shall in Love delight.
Nor a thorn nor a threat stain her beauty bright.

# Infant Joy

I have no name
I am but two days old.—
What shall I call thee?
I happy am
Joy is my name,—
Sweet joy befall thee!

Pretty joy!
Sweet joy but two days old.
Sweet joy I call thee;
Thou dost smile.
I sing the while
Sweet joy befall thee.

# 6    The Role of Childhood

One of the most significant influences on late eighteenth-century thought about education was the philosopher Jean-Jacques Rousseau, whose key works *Of the Social Contract* and *Emile, or, on Education* were both published in 1762. Rousseau argued that all human beings are born with an innate sensitivity to virtue, which urban European civilisation tends to suppress; political authorities impose restrictive conformity on individuals, stifling their essential goodness and producing – in Rousseau's eyes – much of the injustice and suffering he saw surrounding him in eighteenth-century society. In its place, Rousseau called for a philosophy of "natural feeling", whereby societies would truly allow each individual to cultivate their "innate principle of justice and virtue". Only this synthesis of natural feeling and overarching social structures could liberate humanity from the loss of happiness and freedom, as intimated in Rousseau's most famous dictum, "Man was born free, and everywhere he is in chains."

Blake's *Songs* cannot be read as an embodiment of Rousseau's ideas – their views diverge in many important respects. But the ideas about education espoused by Rousseau significantly shape Blake's presentation of childhood in particular. For the most part, Blake depicts childhood positively and affectionately, as a time in which human beings are more purely attuned to their own natural instincts and unhindered by the artificial impositions of urban society. The *Songs of Innocence* are rich with a sense of childhood as a state of spiritual energy. In "The School Boy", for instance, the child of the title is initially shown to be happy within the freedom and beauty of nature:

I love to rise in a summer morn,
When the birds sing on every tree;
The distant huntsman winds his horn,
And the skylark sings with me.
Oh! What sweet company.

The boy's singing with the skylark displays a oneness between the child and nature that eradicates any sense of isolation – the boy is not alone, as nature itself provides "sweet company". The adult huntsman is the only ambiguous figure within this scene – a threat to nature, but mercifully "distant", allowing the boy's communion with the natural world to take place unimpeded. It is the presence of "school", in the next stanza, which "drives all joy away". The word "joy" is repeated throughout the poem, symbolising the free happiness that school obliterates. The boy himself becomes a bird, emphasising his unity with nature in a metaphor that presents formal education as a kind of spiritual imprisonment: "How can the bird that is born for joy/Sit in a cage and sing?" Here the "cage" symbolises the entrapping schoolroom, but also perhaps the body, with the "bird" symbolising the boy's soul or imaginative spirit. Crucially – in another reflection of Rousseau's ideas – learning itself is also disrupted by school:

Ah! Then at times I drooping sit,
And spend many an anxious hour,
Nor in my book can I take delight,
Nor sit in learning's bower,
Worn through with the dreary shower.

The boy yearns here to take "delight" in learning and his books, but is thwarted by the stultifying effect of school education, underlined by the oppressive language of "drooping", "anxious", and "dreary". Implicitly, in this poem, it is the boy's parents who are to blame: the boy pleads to his "father and mother" not to let him be "blown away" in such a manner, as Blake challenges institutional education and parents' passive acceptance of their children's spiritual suffocation at the hands of the "cruel eye" of school, envisaged here as a vehicle for surveillance and hostile scrutiny.

"The School Boy" exemplifies Blake's scepticism about formal education at the same time as it celebrates the natural freedoms of childhood. Throughout *Innocence*, childhood – in its unthreatened state – is emphasised as a time not only of "innocence" and purity, but also of unique happiness. In "A Cradle Song", a mother keeps vigil over her sleeping baby:

> Sleep, sleep happy child.
> All creation slept and smiled.
> Sleep, sleep, happy sleep,
> While o'er thee thy mother weep.

There is an obvious contrast here between the happy sleep of the child, and the weeping of the mother; as is often the case in the *Songs*, the source and meaning of this weeping is ambiguous, and it could signify either joy or despair. The possibility of the latter is inescapable: this apparently exultant poem is imbued with an underlying sense of discomfort as a result, the peaceful slumber of the child painfully juxtaposed with a grieving adult presence. Essick notes, too, that there are "discordant elements" to the poem's accompanying image; the scene of mother and child appears "claustrophobic, with heavy clothing, covered hair, dark shadows", the child displays no "bodily evidence of joyous energy", and there is perhaps even "a threatening aspect to the mother's posture, one that expresses anxiety as much as love" (Essick 60). The overall movement of the poem, though, is clearly one of celebration. Towards the end of the poem, the child is deified, becoming at one with God himself in another emphatic indication of Blake's belief in the unique holiness and spirituality of early life: "Sweet babe, in thy face/Holy image I can trace// ... Infant smiles are his own smiles".

A similar sense of jubilation is evident in "Infant Joy", where the new-born child sings "I happy am/Joy is my name", expressing a pure, affirmative "joy" that seems once again to embody the idea of childhood as a time of unadulterated spiritual and emotional wholesomeness, notably distinct from the complicated emotional realities of adulthood. The fact that this child is "but two days old" – together with the origin of "infant" in the Latin *in-fans*, unable to speak – suggests that the joy the child expresses here is, paradoxically, a form of inarticulate rapture beyond the human language it will eventually learn. Throughout the *Songs of Innocence*, joy seems to represent a state of pure bliss – an uncomplicated happiness hinted at in the "Introduction", with its concluding hope that "Every child may joy to hear" these *Songs*.

It is only in the light of *Experience* that this meaning to the word "joy" begins to warp before our eyes. In "The Sick Rose", the "invisible worm/that flies in the night//Has found out thy bed of crimson joy"; here, "joy" appears to have sexual implications, with the rose a symbol of feminine loss of innocence and the worm a phallic symbol of threatening male desire. In "The Garden of Love", the poet observes that priests in their "black gowns" are "binding with briars" his "joys and desires"; here, "joy" seems to be associated with natural human impulses, the desires of the body as well as the spirit, locked in combat with the oppressive doctrines of the Christian Church as espoused by the priest. Looking back at "Infant Joy" in the light of the other poems from *Experience*, questions begin to emerge over how purely innocent the "joy" there really is. What kind of shadow might experience cast over this apparently blissful scene? The word "befall" in the final line perhaps echoes the Fall from Edenic innocence into a corrupt world; the apparently exultant wish, "sweet joy befall thee", could perhaps even be a reference to the far-from-innocent pleasures that inevitably await this child in the course of its life. The image accompanying the poem seems, moreover, to depict an impassive-faced infant who displays none of the joy the poem expresses; in addition, the angel hovering over the baby seems deliberately placed to suggest the stamen of the flower in which the trio sit, conjuring up ideas of reproduction at the same time as the poem appears to celebrate the newborn infant's freedom from the sexual impulses of the adult world.

Childhood is, therefore, clearly a key component of Blake's complex vision of innocence – not synonymous with it, but closely associated. The underbelly of the purity of childhood is its vulnerability, and Blake frequently draws attention to the frailty of children in the *Songs of Innocence*. The state of childhood itself, whilst it requires protection, is generally devoid of overt corruption in these *Innocence* poems, but when we turn to the *Songs of Experience* the picture becomes more complicated. Ultimately, it becomes impossible to define Blake's overall perspective as one of a clear-cut opposition between childhood purity and corrupt adulthood. As always, Blake's system of contraries means that opposing perspectives are offered as counterbalancing forces in the dramatic tensions of the overall work. In the poems of *Experience*, childhood is not always portrayed in such pure terms – such as in "Infant Sorrow":

> My mother groaned, my father wept,
> Into the dangerous world I leapt;
> Helpless, naked, piping loud,
> Like a fiend hid in a cloud.
>
> Struggling in my father's hands,
> Striving against my swaddling bands,
> Bound and weary, I thought best
> To sulk upon my mother's breast.

Here, the newborn infant appears to be malign, even evil, from the moment of birth – an absolute contrast to the baby's pure happiness in "Infant Joy". The mother's groans suggest the pain of childbirth, and perhaps hint too at an emotional despair in the aftermath of labour. Again we encounter an ambiguously weeping parent – in this case the father – but the overall atmosphere of discord lends weight to an interpretation of these tears as a reflection of the "sorrow" of the title. The child's "piping" ironically echoes the piping of the poet in the "Introduction" to *Innocence*, but with the music replaced here by the baby's frustrated cries. The child explicitly compares itself to a "fiend", suggesting a satanic quality, an innate evil which once again might be perceived as a positive energy: as a counter-image of "Infant Joy", this poem emphasises the presence of corruption and destructive energy in all human beings, hinting again at man's fallen-ness and at the inevitability of suffering. This is the "dangerous" world of experience, in which the adult figures will not reliably provide any comfort or protection.

The overall feeling in this poem is one of struggle and spite, and it offers an important complicating dimension to any consideration of childhood and its presentation in the *Songs* as a whole. The shift from *Innocence* to *Experience* is not a shift from childhood to adulthood, but instead more of a shift between competing visions of how childhood itself might be understood. A worldview of experience cannot sustain the untainted view of childhood delivered in *Innocence*, and so childhood itself becomes darkened, more ambiguously described. A useful example of this can be found in the two "Nurse's Song" poems. In its *Innocence* rendering, the children are shown to be "laughing" on the hill, and the nurse, after a gentle request that they "come home", allows them to play longer "till the light fades away". The justification that the children offer for remaining outside underlines their jubilation, as well as suggesting a communion with nature evocative of "The School Boy":

> No, no, let us play, for it is yet day
> And we cannot go to sleep.
> Besides, in the sky the little birds fly
> And the hills are all covered with sheep.

The sense here is clearly of childhood as a time of happiness, freedom, and profound oneness with the natural environment. In the "Nurse's Song" of *Experience*, the nurse's reaction to the children's play is markedly different, as her face turns "green and pale" with envious recollection of her own, lost youth. This adds a bite of possible resentment to her request of "come home, my children". But the children's activity is itself depicted differently here; they engage in "whisperings", not laughing, suggestive of subterfuge and secrecy. The nurse claims "Your spring and your day are wasted in play, your winter and night in disguise" – an ambiguous ending which suggests either that the children's innocence will inevitably end, replaced by the corrupt "winter and night" of adulthood, or that there is a hidden level of "disguise" and deceit within childhood itself.

In any case, it is not simply the tone of this poem that differs from its counterpart in *Innocence*, but the vision of childhood it depicts. The dramatic framework of the *Songs* again allows Blake to deliver contradictory perspectives which sit alongside each other as part of a conflicted and disjointed portrait of humanity – a melting-pot of conflicting states, with each Song embodying a flawed, incomplete perspective upon the world. As Jonathan Roberts notes, it was Blake's belief that "to escape states of error … we first need to recognize them, and art is a means of doing this because it is able to embody them. Once we have embodied error by giving it form, we can cast it out."

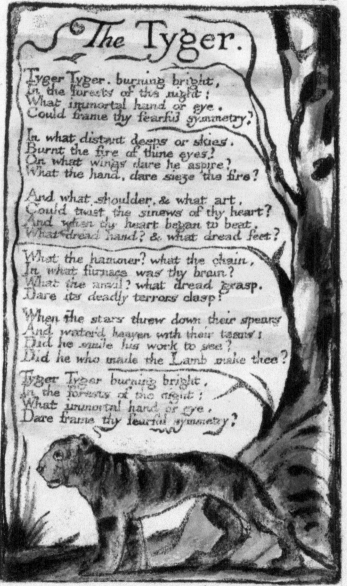

# The Tyger.

Tyger Tyger. burning bright,
In the forests of the night:
What immortal hand or eye.
Could frame thy fearful symmetry?

In what distant deeps or skies.
Burnt the fire of thine eyes?
On what wings dare he aspire?
What the hand, dare sieze the fire?

And what shoulder, & what art,
Could twist the sinews of thy heart?
And when thy heart began to beat,
What dread hand? & what dread feet?

What the hammer? what the chain,
In what furnace was thy brain?
What the anvil? what dread grasp,
Dare its deadly terrors clasp!

When the stars threw down their spears
And water'd heaven with their tears:
Did he smile his work to see?
Did he who made the Lamb make thee?

Tyger Tyger burning bright,
In the forests of the night:
What immortal hand or eye,
Dare frame thy fearful symmetry?

# 7   Blake's Visual Images

For publishers and poetry anthologists, Blake's unique methods present something of a problem. Any printing of his original plates is relatively complicated, and relatively expensive; it is much easier, and much cheaper, to publish his work in a text-only format. This purely practical issue is one reason why the words of Blake's art have so often been detached from the images that originally accompanied them. Despite the wonderful breakthrough in this area represented by the William Blake Archive online, this remains a thorny issue surrounding publications of Blake's work.

To read any of Blake's work without attention to its visual dimensions, though, is to misread it. "I know myself both Poet & Painter", he wrote in an 1803 letter to Thomas Butts. The breaking apart of these verbal and visual elements pushes against the fundamental texture and philosophy of Blake's project. It is worth remembering that Blake's title page for the *Songs of Innocence and of Experience* describes them as being by "The Author & Printer W Blake". The words "author" and "printer" are curious choices that suggest much about how Blake saw himself. "Author" significantly encompasses both the written and the visual aspects of his art – Blake is not simply a "poet" or "writer", but a creator of compositions that cannot be confined by terms denoting only the production of text. Of equal importance is Blake's decision to describe himself as a "printer", a word that simultaneously signposts Blake's trade as an engraver, the fact these *Songs* are published by Blake himself, and the unusual published format of the work. Blake's methods of engraving the plates, of painstakingly printing the reliefs and then hand-painting each design, are part of the fundamental fabric of his artistic invention, and cannot be ignored by anyone seeking a full understanding of his artistic endeavour. The *Songs* are an intricate intermingling of image and text, and it is not possible to understand them adequately without attempting to "read" both of these elements alongside each other.

An excellent example of this point can be found in "The Tyger", a poem whose mysteries and ambiguities only seem to deepen further upon examination of the surprising image Blake created as its accompaniment. As always, the fine details of the image vary from copy to copy, making any all-encompassing interpretation impossible. But there is no escaping the bizarre, almost comic nature of Blake's picture of the "tyger". Underneath his description of its incomprehensible ferocity and fearsome power, there appears a fearful, rather gormless creature, almost more like a domestic cat than the wild creature the poem describes. This image has drawn the attention, and the confusion, of many critics. It has been proposed, for instance, that Blake simply wasn't any good at drawing tigers; Peter Ackroyd, for instance, suggests its incompetence might "be simply an example of his inability to depict anything other than the human form" (Ackroyd 147). This proposition, though, feels defective in the light of Blake's ample artistic credentials and the complexity and magnificence of many of his other images, including animals; his engraving of the pilgrims in Chaucer's *The Canterbury Tales*, for example, includes some highly intricate and skilled depictions of horses.

Equally difficult to sustain, though, is the idea that the image *does* in fact look intimidating: there is no surviving copy of the *Songs* that displays this tiger as anything other than a comic shadow of its verbal counterpart. A more plausible interpretation is offered by Susan Wolfson, who suggests that the inadequacy of the picture relates to the difficulty of "framing" the tiger, of successfully taming its sublimity into an understandable and observable visual form: the pictured tiger, she writes, is "either mocking the questioner's anxiety with contradiction, or mocking us, with false safety" (Wolfson, "Blake's Language", 72). It may also be that the picture displays how the tiger looks from the perspective of innocence. Whatever one's view, the image unavoidably shifts our perceptions of the poem, deepening the already complicated questions surrounding the nature of Blake's tiger and what it might represent: the image is part of the work, and any analysis of the poem that fails to take the image into account is, therefore, inevitably both distorted and incomplete.

The image accompanying "The Tyger" is in a sense unusual, in that it so obviously appears to contradict the message and description of the poem. More commonly, the images seem – at least on the surface – to complement Blake's words in an appropriate manner. There is always, though, some kind of shift, a new illumination of Blake's meaning. In "The Blossom", Blake appears to be describing the unity between the speaker and living forms of the natural world:

Merry Merry Sparrow
Under leaves so green
A happy Blossom
Sees you swift as arrow
Seek your cradle narrow
Near my Bosom.

The sense of innocence and purity here is perhaps complicated by the evidently phallic connotations of the "arrow" simile, and the vaginal connotations of "cradle narrow": the stanza *could* be read as embodying the untainted unity of innocence, or as a metaphor for sex – or perhaps as an intermingling of the two, a presentation of sexual union in pure and celebratory terms. Essick points out that "A blossom is, after all, the reproductive organ of a plant, and the use of flower imagery as a metaphor for human female sexuality is indicated by terms such as 'deflowering'" (Essick 36).

The accompanying image lends weight to this sexual interpretation, as it depicts a fiery blossom surging up the right-hand side of the plate, supporting the phallic implications in the text. Winged seraphim float round its upper leaves, suggesting procreative possibility, with one of them cradled by an adult female: an emblem, perhaps, of the moment of successful fertilisation. The image, in other words, does not contradict the text so much as highlight and emphasise certain aspects that are already to some extent evident. In the poem's second stanza, the "sobbing" of the Robin perhaps hints at the distress of lost sexual innocence in a manner that points towards its contrary poem in *Experience*, "The Sick Rose".

The subtle ways in which Blake's images can influence our reading of the poems can be as slight, and as difficult to pin down, as the specific hue of paint used on a particular copy. The fact that Blake and his wife hand-painted each page means that the details of the paintwork vary between editions. As a result, different versions of the same plate – and as a consequence, numerous different possible threads of meaning – simultaneously exist, depending on the copy one is looking at. In a poem as seemingly joyous as "The Lamb", for instance, the background sky is sometimes infused with an ominous, blackish purple. Could this hint at the encroaching presence of experience within this tranquil scene? The precise quality of the colour differs, of course, depending on the copy, and this inevitably affects how persuasive such a reading might be. Similar ambiguities can be found in the different copies of "The Shepherd", where the darkness of the sky again perhaps indicates the threatening world of experience from which the shepherd protects his flock. In the image that accompanies the *Songs of Experience* title page – a man with winged child on his shoulders, perhaps confrontationally stalking towards the reader – the surrounding sky is a reddish hue, suggesting evening and decline, perhaps even hinting at something satanic and infernal that anticipates the fallen, broken world of experience. All readings of this kind, though, are tied up in the fine details of particular colours used on particular copies – rich with meaning, but painfully elusive, and impossible to use as the basis for any generalised interpretation.

In the end, even this effort to bring together Blake's words and images does not adequately recognise the importance of his original plates. The text itself, in its original printed form, is alive with significance – changing appearance in various ways from plate to plate, and often surrounded by decorative motifs that are charged with meaning. In the title plate to the *Songs of Innocence*, for instance, the word "Songs" directly blooms out of a tree below, highlighting the close association Blake wishes to explore between the state of innocence and the natural world. In numerous Songs from *Innocence* – the "Introduction", "The Ecchoing Green", "A Cradle Song", "Spring", "Nurse's Song", and others – the title and sometimes the words of the poems spring out from surrounding tendrils and branches, giving the impression that the poems are part of the fabric of nature itself.

In *Experience*, the words tend to be more distinct from the surrounding decorative designs, and often appear in plainer, bolder text. Little strokes and flourishes surround many Songs, often hinting at something more than mere ornamentation. In some – such as "Nurse's Song" and "Holy Thursday" from *Innocence* – undulating lines of varying lengths run between the lines of the poem, suggesting something rhythmical, a suggested beat or metre for the verse. The American poet, Allen Ginsberg, understood these lines as a loose form of musical notation, and amongst other things they are another reminder of the close association between these *Songs* and music. Most of all, though, they are a reminder that any proper attention to the *Songs* must involve close attention to Blake's original plates. All aspects of each plate – the words, the images, the decorative embellishments, and the hand-painted backgrounds – contribute to the overall meaning, and the removal of them from many editions of Blake's verse has inevitably diminished the power and warped the sense that the work possesses in its original form. According to Stephen Behrendt, "Blake's illuminated poems generate what is essentially a 'third text', a meta-text that partakes of both the verbal and the visual texts, but that is neither the sum of, nor identical with either of, those two texts" (Behrendt, "The 'Third Text'", 549). Blake's fusion of word and image creates an alchemical reaction that lends the *Songs* a uniquely multi-dimensional power, as they become ambiguous multiple texts that are more than the sum of their component parts; to sunder words from images, as many editors have done, is inevitably to remove the *Songs* of their unique mystery.

# HOLY THURSDAY

Twas on a Holy Thursday their innocent faces clean
The children walking two & two in red & blue & green
Grey headed beadles walkd before with wands as white as snow
Till into the high dome of Pauls they like Thames waters flow

O what a multitude they seemd these flowers of London town
Seated in companies they sit with radiance all their own
The hum of multitudes was there but multitudes of lambs
Thousands of little boys & girls raising their innocent hands

Now like a mighty wind they raise to heaven the voice of song
Or like harmonious thunderings the seats of heaven among
Beneath them sit the aged men wise guardians of the poor
Then cherish pity, lest you drive an angel from your door

# Laughing Song.

When the green woods laugh with the voice of joy,
And the dimpling stream runs laughing by,
When the air does laugh with our merry wit,
And the green hill laughs with the noise of it.

When the meadows laugh with lively green,
And the grasshopper laughs in the merry scene,
When Mary and Susan and Emily,
With their sweet round mouths sing Ha Ha He.

When the painted birds laugh in the shade
Where our table with cherries and nuts is spread
Come live & be merry and join with me,
To sing the sweet chorus of Ha Ha He.

# 8    Why Are They Called "Songs"?

"Music rots when it gets too far from the dance. Poetry atrophies when it gets too far from music", wrote Ezra Pound in his *ABC of Reading*. The relationship between song and poetry has a long history, but there is enough curiosity surrounding Blake's use of the word "song" to merit some careful attention. Why, exactly, did Blake call them songs, not poems? One answer evidently lies in Blake's ties to the religious literature of the period, as well as his use of the Bible – especially the Psalms. The influence of eighteenth-century hymns, and instructional volumes like Watts' *Divine Songs for Children*, brings to light important links between the *Songs* and music; Blake's use of form in the *Songs* is also significantly influenced by the formal structures of the hymns so popular throughout the century. Profoundly opposed to the established Church, Blake nevertheless wished to infuse his work with a strong sense of the devotional, replacing what he saw as the oppressive phenomenon of traditional church worship with his own forms of spiritual celebration.

Many *Songs* explicitly associate singing with the expression of spiritual joy. "How can the bird that is born for joy/Sit in a cage and Sing?", bemoans "The School Boy"; and in "Holy Thursday" from *Innocence*, the singing of a poverty-stricken St Paul's congregation is described in rousing terms: "Thousands of little boys & girls raising their innocent hands//Now like a mighty wind they raise to heaven the voice of song". As much as Blake despised the established Church and traditional doctrine, then, he exploited the traditional Christian idea of song as an opening up of the soul, providing potential access to the divine ("The pastures are clothed with flocks; the valleys also are covered over with corn; they shout for joy, they also sing", Psalm 65).

Throughout his life, Blake certainly seemed to perceive his own poetry as intimately linked to music and singing. A contemporary, writing about a gathering of writers at the house of Harriet Mathew, describes seeing Blake "read and sing several of his poems". There is evidence to suggest that Blake chanted and sung much of his earlier verse to friends and fellow artists, and the influence of music upon the *Songs* is substantial. Some seem quite clearly to be intended for musical accompaniment, such as "Laughing Song":

When the painted birds laugh in the shade
Where our table with cherries and nuts is spread
Come live & be merry and join with me,
To sing the sweet chorus of Ha, Ha, He.

Here, the activity of laughter – often linked with joy, childhood freedom, and oneness with nature, as in "Nurse's Song" ("The little ones leaped and shouted and laughed/And all the hills echoed") – is tangled up with the activity of singing in an expression of merriment and harmony. The simplicity of the language, and the explicit references to music, have promoted a sense amongst critics that Blake specifically intended this poem to be sung. Geoffrey Keynes describes this poem as "literally a song for singing", and proposes that "'the sweet chorus of Ha, Ha, He' calls for a simple, merry tune". Other poems in *Innocence*, such as "Spring", contain a similar lyrical simplicity that suggests these poems as literally "songs", verbal templates upon which music and melody should be imposed.

If, at one level, "song" for Blake meant spiritual celebration, this certainly does not suffice as an explanation of song's meaning and purpose in the work as a whole. In *Experience*, singing is more often conspicuous by its absence, or weaved into a tirade against social injustice, as in "Holy Thursday":

Is this a holy thing to see,
In a rich and fruitful land,
Babes reduced to misery,
Fed with cold and usurious hand?

> Is that trembling cry a song?
> Can it be a song of joy?
> And so many children poor?
> It is a land of poverty!

In contrast to its contrary poem in *Innocence*, the congregation here are unable to produce a "song of joy"; their weakened efforts instead convey their poverty, suffering, and misery. Here lies a key difference between the states of innocence and experience: in the latter, social injustice interferes with spiritual possibility. Even the buoyancy and optimism of "Holy Thursday" in *Innocence* is potentially undermined by that lyric's original appearance as a satirical piece in Blake's *Poetical Sketches* (1784). Versions of two other *Innocence* Songs – "The Little Boy Lost" and "Nurse's Song" – also first appeared in the same collection, and the extent to which this original satirical context hangs over their presence in *Innocence* has been a matter of considerable critical debate.

In the *Songs of Experience*, Blake refashions the meaning of "song" so that it becomes something bleaker and angrier, a lament for absent spirituality more than a celebration of its presence. In the last stanza of "The Chimney Sweeper", the boy laments the blindness of his parents to his own suffering:

> And because I am happy, & dance, & sing,
> They think they have done me no injury:
> And are gone to praise God & his Priest & King
> Who make up a heaven of our misery.

Here, curiously, the sweeper's happiness seems to survive his pain – coexisting with his suffering, but not cancelling it out. His dancing and singing is presented as an emblem of his innocence, indestructible despite the awfulness of his predicament. The description of the boy's parents at church again highlights Blake's contempt for institutionalised religion, and his belief that the "God" worshipped by Christians was a false God, an oppressive ruler, antithetical to the kinds of spiritual freedom Blake sought.

The word "song" in the *Songs of Innocence and of Experience* thus becomes a rather slippery and intriguing term, far more complicated and difficult to pin down than simply a substitute term for poetry. In *Experience*, it appears to evolve a more ironic meaning, as Blake's poems express worldviews more sceptical about the joys of *Innocence* – they are, paradoxically, songs that critique the idea of song as an emblem of connectedness to spirituality and joy. Throughout the *Songs*, Blake explores the complex tensions between song and poetry – between spoken and written forms of communication. The introductions to each collection can be read, amongst other things, as a play on this idea. In the "Introduction" to *Innocence*, the child-muse "wept with joy" at the poet's music, but vanishes when he starts to write; in the "Introduction" to *Experience*, the command to "Hear the voice of the Bard" is instantly undermined by the impossibility of *hearing* any written text. As the poet Glyn Maxwell has recently put it, "Songs are strung upon sounds, poems upon silence" (Maxwell 13): the link between song and poetry is also a schism, an unbridgeable gulf between sonic and silent utterance, the sound of speech versus the soundlessness of text. Blake was well aware that the plates he was creating were destined to exist in the soundless space of the printed page. In this sense, "songs" is a deliberate and provocative misnomer: Blake's *Songs* cannot be "songs" in any true or complete sense without the reader completing the process, by resurrecting the silence of the text on the page into some verbalised form of music and melody.

Leopards, tygers play,
Round her as she lay;
While the lion old,
Bow'd his mane of gold,

And her bosom lick,
And upon her neck,
From his eyes of flame,
Ruby tears there came;

While the lioness
Loos'd her slender dress,
And naked they convey'd
To caves the sleeping maid.

# The Little Girl Found

All the night in woe,
Lyca's parents go:
Over vallies deep.
While the desarts weep.

Tired and woe-begone,
Hoarse with making moan:
Arm in arm seven days,
They traed the desart ways.

Seven nights they sleep,
Among shadows deep:
And dream they see their child
Starv'd in desart wild.

Pale thro' pathless ways
The fancied image strays,

Famish'd

# The Little Girl Lost

In futurity
I prophetic see.
That the earth from sleep.
(Grave the sentence deep)

Shall arise and seek
For her maker meek:
And the desart wild,
Become a garden mild.

In the southern clime,
Where the summers prime,
Never fades away;
Lovely Lyca lay.

Seven summers old
Lovely Lyca told,
She had wanderd long,
Hearing wild birds song.

Sweet sleep come to me
Underneath this tree;
Do father, mother weep.—
Where can Lyca sleep.

Lost in desart wild
Is your little child.
How can Lyca sleep,
If her mother weep.

If her heart does ake,
Then let Lyca wake;
If my mother sleep,
Lyca shall not weep,

Frowning frowning night,
O'er this desart bright.
Let thy moon arise,
While I close my eyes.

Sleeping Lyca lay;
While the beasts of prey,
Come from caverns deep,
Viewd the maid asleep

The kingly lion stood
And the virgin viewd,
Then he gambold round
O'er the hallowd ground:

## 9   Could Blake Spell?

Blake received little formal education, and his tirades against school – together with the many accounts of his stubborn and anti-authoritarian character – suggest it would have been very difficult for anyone to teach Blake but himself. "Thank God I never was sent to school/To be flogd into following the style of a fool", he once wrote. He is one of the great autodidacts of literary history, studying with extraordinary range and intensity from a very young age – in an 1803 letter to William Hayley, he described himself as "A Man almost 50 Years of Age, who has not lost any of his life since he was five years old without incessant labour & study". Throughout his adult life, this puritanical work ethic crucially fed itself into the highly laborious work of sketching, engraving, and painting his plates, even though times were often hard and sales of his work painfully inconsistent.

It can be tempting to view some of the idiosyncrasies of Blake's writing – odd spellings, twisted syntax, sparse punctuation – as simply a product of his limited schooling; quirks that would have been ironed out of him by a more orthodox education. It is worth remembering, too, that in the late eighteenth century there was a far less standardised understanding of English spellings, despite the appearance of Samuel Johnson's unprecedentedly wide-ranging and detailed dictionary in 1755. But these oddities that run throughout Blake's work, including the *Songs*, often feel like something more – a deliberate aspect of his intention, rather than just accident or eccentricity. There has, for instance, been some considerable debate over Blake's spelling of "The Tyger". Is there any significance to be gleaned from his use of a "y" here? The extent to which this is a deviant spelling is itself a difficult question. It certainly appears, to a contemporary reader, to be so; but in the late eighteenth century, "official" spellings were far less securely settled, and other uses of "tyger" as a spelling can be found in literature of the period.

Intriguingly, Blake's own writing itself fails to provide a consistent picture. Towards the end of his enigmatic visionary poem *Europe*, he writes "The Tigers couch upon the prey & suck the ruddy tide"; elsewhere, though, he deploys the same variant "y" spelling, as in *The Marriage of Heaven and Hell*: "The tygers of wrath are wiser than the horses of destruction". Do such variations indicate that Blake intended his "tyger" with a "y" to represent not the physical animal, but something else, a metaphorical beast emblematic of power, rage, and vitality? Some critics have seen it this way. Nelson Hilton proposes that it "could have been spelled, as Blake does elsewhere, with an 'i' except that it is not about a 'tiger' any more than *The Lamb*, on whose reverse it is etched, concerns a young sheep" (Hilton, "Blake's Early Works", 207). The apparently simple matter of Blake's spelling becomes one of the mysteries of the poem, beguiling the reader into a tortuous consideration of its potential significance, or insignificance.

Similarly tempting readings hover over Blake's other eccentrically spelled words in the *Songs*. There frequently appears to be a notable appropriateness, a pertinent significance to his mis-spellings when they occur. The very question of whether Blake intended these mis-spellings to be significant is itself one that a reader may or may not wish to consider relevant: significant strains of literary theory, influenced by the ideas of post-structuralists such as Roland Barthes and Jacques Derrida, proclaim the irrelevance of authorial intention to the processes of reading and analysis. The writer's hand, claims Barthes in a famous essay entitled "The Death of the Author", "traces a field without origin – or which, at least, has no other origin than language itself, language which ceaselessly calls into question all origins" (Barthes 146). If meaning is there in the *text*, in other words, perhaps Blake's conscious intentions – or lack of them – are not something we even need to consider.

Sometimes, it must be said, direct significance to a particular spelling is more overt and convincing than at others. The presence of the double "c" in "The Ecchoing Green", for instance, is of unmistakeable import. The doubled letter signifies the process of echoing that the poem describes, a textual embodiment of the harmonious reverberations of the natural world and the people making merry within it. Elsewhere, the mis-spellings look intriguing and provocative, but are more questionable as a basis for analytical consideration. One example appears in "The Little Girl Lost", when Lyca is described as "lost in desart wild":

> Lost in desart wild
> Is your little child.
> How can Lyca sleep,
> If her mother weep.
>
> If her heart does ake,
> Then let Lyca wake;
> If my mother sleep,
> Lyca shall not weep.
>
> Frowning frowning night,
> O'er this desart bright
> Let thy moon arise,
> While I close my eyes.

The spelling of "ache" as "ake" here seems nothing more than a variant spelling, with no obvious thematic significance. But the spelling of "desert" as "desart" is more intriguing. Could the presence of "art" within the word "desart" be of any importance? It is, again, the kind of reading that has sometimes attracted critics, drawn as they are by the inscrutability of Blake to the smallest details of his work. "The Little Girl Lost" occupies an ambiguous middle ground in the narrative of the *Songs*: Blake originally included it in *Innocence*, but later

63

switched it to *Experience*. As a landscape of experience, where the girl will be seduced by the "beasts of prey", this "desart wild" could be figured as in direct contrast to the "valleys wild" of *Innocence*. Rather than being a place of imaginative inspiration, it is a barren des*art* in which art is absent, leaving the abandoned girl vulnerable to violation, to the loss of innocence.

This reading, though – while appealing – feels inevitably weakened by the extent to which "desart" as a variant of "desert" was so widespread in eighteenth-century English. But the urge remains forensically to examine the details of these poems in an effort to unpick their secrets, and this does not simply relate to Blake's sometimes curious spellings. His punctuation and syntax are equally unorthodox at times, in a manner that must significantly affect any careful reading. Blake rarely deploys quotation marks, creating the effect of distinct voices in each poem merging into each other, as in the "Introduction" to *Innocence*, "Infant Joy", "Nurse's Song", "The Clod and the Pebble", and "A Little Boy Lost". In "The Lamb", the absence of question marks in the opening lines – "Little Lamb who made thee/Dost thou know who made thee" – allows them to feel like statements, not questions, extinguishing any sense of doubt about the divine origin and nature of the Lamb. Notably, in its contrary poem, "The Tyger", Blake does deploy question marks – a total of eleven, throughout the poem – adding to its atmosphere of uncertainty and fear.

Elsewhere, in "The Little Black Boy", the speaker laments his black skin – perceiving it as disturbingly inconsistent with the purity and whiteness of his soul – but is comforted by his mother's vision of the brevity of life and the boy's emancipation from the "cloud" of his body. In the final stanzas, the little black boy apparently seeks to befriend a white English boy by proposing that they will both soon find joy together beyond death:

> Thus did my mother say and kissed me.
> And thus I say to little English boy.

When I from black and he from white cloud free,
And round the tent of God like Lambs we joy:

Ill shade him from the heat till he can bear,
To lean in joy upon our fathers knee.
And then I'll stand and stroke his silver hair,
And be like him and he will then love me.

The sentiment here appears to be one of generosity and straightforward spiritual optimism. But the lack of an apostrophe in the "Ill" of "Ill shade him" hints at a secondary meaning. Could the boy resentfully be imagining the English boy's pain and discomfort, in a manner that problematises the warmth of his feelings? Hilton suggests that the "omitted apostrophe ... makes the black boy echo conventional malediction in imagining 'Ill shade him', even as he fantasises the unreal 'silver hair' for the white boy and, pathetically, the concluding wan hope that he will finally 'be like him and he will then love me'" (Hilton 201). It might seem, on the surface, to be a tenuous reading, but it is strengthened by Blake's use of an apostrophe in "I'll stand" just two lines later. The two words stand in stark contrast to each other, encouraging us to read "Ill shade him" not simply as a moment of odd punctuation, but an indication of half-buried malice.

This form of approach to an interpretation of the *Songs* is contested territory. Some dismiss these kinds of typographically oriented readings as too shaky and speculative – reflective more of Blake's own eccentricity and educational history than of anything useful in the work itself. But one should guard against a caricatured vision of Blake as an ill-educated maverick; his feverish studies brought him into contact with a wide range of literature and philosophy, far too much for any idea of Blake's intellectual isolation to be adequate. The dismissal of the typographical oddities of the *Songs* feels, on balance, rather too easy, and inconsistent with the ferocity of Blake's own vision, his obsessive attention to minutiae, and his evident delight in mystery.

# The Blossom

Merry Merry Sparrow
Under leaves so green
A happy Blossom
Sees you swift as arrow
Seek your cradle narrow
Near my Bosom .

Pretty Pretty Robin
Under leaves so green
A happy Blossom
Hears you sobbing sobbing
Pretty Pretty Robin
Near my Bosom .

## 10   Was Blake a Romantic Poet?

It has become customary for Blake to be considered a
Romantic poet. Whether this is a fair or accurate label to
impose upon him, though, is a vexed question. Critics and
scholars often show a tendency to tidy up literary history, finding patterns amongst the chaos of individual writers' lives and
sorting them into particular groups or movements which can
then be more easily defined and analysed. But this approach
can involve distortion, the imposition of false coherences on
the complex and disordered landscape of literature within
any particular historical period. As David Simpson, author
of a penetrating essay on Blake and Romanticism, puts it,
"writers tend not to live, publish, and die at times that fit
neatly into latterday critical schemata" (Simpson, "Blake and
Romanticism", 170).

There is no doubt that Romanticism has been the movement to which Blake has most frequently been attached.
Anthologies of Romantic verse almost invariably include
Blake's work, occasionally under a qualifying sub-heading
such as "early Romantic" or "pre-Romantic". Northrop Frye,
seeing the shakiness of this connection, tried to shift opinion
by constructing a context he termed "the age of Blake", but the
dragging of Blake into discussions of Romanticism remains
popular. He has often been talked about, and written about,
alongside William Wordsworth and Samuel Coleridge in particular, as if a coherent ideology binds these figures together
in a manner that makes the umbrella term "Romantic" a convincing one with which to describe all of them.

But was Blake, in any meaningful sense, a Romantic
poet? What, in any case, does being a "Romantic poet" mean?

Simpson emphasises that the term usually suggests not simply a particular period, but a shared set of ideas and concerns:

> To call a writer Romantic has ... traditionally been to signal an interest in such categories as genius, nature, childhood, and imagination, perhaps along with some assumed response to the French Revolution. Those who wrote in the Romantic period but wrote about other things or demonstrated other priorities have then come to be, oddly, not Romantic in this particular sense. (Simpson 170)

Any overall definition of Romanticism is evidently an awkward matter, but Simpson offers some useful starting-points here for a consideration of key themes. In purely historical terms, Blake only crudely fits the generally agreed parameters of the Romantic period: born in 1757, he was significantly older than the two Romantic poets chronologically closest to him, Wordsworth (born in 1770) and Coleridge (born in 1772), and he hardly crossed paths with either of them throughout his life. In addition, Blake's opinion of Wordsworth's poetry was very mixed. Towards the end of his life, he wrote of one Wordsworth poem ("To H. C. Six Years Old") that "This is all in the highest degree Imaginative & equal to any Poet, but not Superior" – an intriguing, somewhat defensive, but evidently enthusiastic comment which he scribbled by hand in a copy of Wordsworth's verse. In other annotations to the very same copy, though, Blake pours scorn on Wordsworth's veneration of nature, seeing it as a misguided preference for physical rather than spiritual and imaginative realities: "I see in Wordsworth the Natural Man rising up against the Spiritual Man Continually, & then he is No Poet but a Heathen Philosopher at Enmity against all true Poetry or Inspiration", and later, "Wordsworth must know that what he writes Valuable is Not to be found in Nature."

It is certainly true that Blake shares some key interests and concerns with Wordsworth, the poet most often identified to be at the heart of Romanticism as a poetic movement.

The famous epigraph to Wordsworth's "Ode: Intimations of Immortality from Recollections of Early Childhood" runs as follows:

> The Child is Father of the Man;
> And I could wish my days to be
> Bound each to each by natural piety.

The poem as a whole deals with the idea that a particular kind of sensitivity to the surrounding world exists in childhood, but it is one that fades on the journey into adulthood. The poem's opening lines show the poet lamenting his loss of this joyful and transcendent childhood vision of the natural world:

> There was a time when meadow, grove, and stream,
> The earth, and every common sight,
>   To me did seem
>   Apparelled in celestial light,
> The glory and the freshness of a dream.
> It is not now as it hath been of yore; –
>   Turn wheresoe'er I may,
>   By night or day,
> These things which I have seen I now can see no more.

As a result of this diminishment, "The Child is Father of the Man": children possess a particular wisdom and insight that elevates them above adults, who can only hold on to such experiences as a steadily fading set of memories. The child is the adult's guide, an "Eye among the Blind", who gives Wordsworth hope later in the poem that he might sustain a connection to the "celestial light" he sees as embodied in nature: "The thought of our past years in me doth breed/ Perpetual benediction". This all sounds very much like Blake's picture of childhood in the *Songs*, a time of purity and spirituality unburdened by the concerns – what Wordsworth calls the "earthly freight" – of adult life. A version of Wordsworth's vision of childhood as a time of unique spiritual understanding can be found in much of the *Songs of Innocence* in particular, especially in poems like "The School Boy", "Infant Joy", "The Ecchoing Green", "Nurse's Song", and "A Cradle Song".

Before one draws any comfortable conclusions, though, it is important to bear several key things in mind about Blake's approach to his own art. Crucially, for a start, the *Songs* are dramatic; for every "Infant Joy", there is an "Infant Sorrow". The system of contraries that Blake believed in and embodied in the *Songs* is radically different to the nostalgic lament for the past delivered by Wordsworth. For Blake, the innocence of childhood must be complicated by the dynamism of experience – in his worldview, any straightforward idea that the shift from childhood to adulthood is a process of loss is not simply insufficient, but wrong. There are differences, too, in their understanding of the moral and spiritual makeup of mankind. In his copy of Wordsworth's poetry, Blake angrily wrote "There is no such thing as Natural Piety as the Natural Man is at Enmity with God." Clearly, he felt Wordsworth's adherence to a traditional Christian understanding of piety to be stultifying, and at odds with the kind of spirituality he so passionately believed in.

Similar differences can be found in the two poets' presentations of nature. Blake's annotations to his copy of Wordsworth's verse make it pretty clear that he had little time for such a doting approach to the natural world. It is worth remembering that, for all his use of pastoral imagery in the *Songs*, he almost never left London, and his relentless attachment to the city of his birth is in stark contrast to Wordsworth and Coleridge's passionate attachment to the Lakes. One of Wordsworth's most famous lyrics, in which he expresses the inspiration he draws from nature, is "I wandered lonely as a cloud", sometimes titled "The Inward Eye". It begins:

> I wandered lonely as a cloud
> That floats on high o'er vales and hills,
> When all at once, I saw a crowd,

> A host, of golden daffodils;
> Beside the lake, beneath the trees,
> Fluttering and dancing in the breeze.

These daffodils, given angelic associations here through the word "host", become for Wordsworth a vision of transcendence and infinitude. This poem perfectly embodies his concept of poetry as "emotion recollected in tranquillity", as he writes of the transformative and palliative effect the memory of these daffodils bring him:

> For oft, when on my couch I lie
> In vacant or in pensive mood,
> They flash upon that inward eye
> That is the bliss of solitude;
> And then my heart with pleasure fills
> And dances with the daffodils.

For Wordsworth, the daffodils provide fire for the "inward eye" of the solitary imagination: here, in a nutshell, is Wordsworth's reverence for nature as an inspirational force upon the individual.

The deep-seated differences between this and Blake's perspective on nature are perhaps best summarised in a lyric Blake wrote in an 1802 letter to Thomas Butts. In it, he outlines a fourfold hierarchy of imaginative vision, and some of his language chimes with that of Wordsworth's poem. He describes walking through a landscape strewn with visions, before encountering a thistle:

> ... before my way
> A frowning Thistle implores my stay.
> What to others a trifle appears
> Fills me full of smiles or tears;
> For double the vision my Eyes do see,
> And a double vision is always with me.
> With my inward eye 'tis an old Man grey;
> With my outward, a Thistle across my way.

71

This description of "double vision" reads like a direct riposte to Wordsworth's poem, but for the fact that this lyric precedes it by two years. For Blake, seeing the thistle simply as itself is immensely limited, a failure of the imagination. His double vision allows him to see it as something entirely different: the lyric becomes a visionary, imaginative dialogue in which he engages the thistle (in its persona as an old man) in an argument that involves the participation of Los, Blake's personified symbol of poetry and the imagination. Blake's poem ends with a description of his perfected "fourfold" vision, in which the limited trappings of reason and physical reality are dispensed with completely in favour of a purely visionary, purely imaginative experience:

> Now I a fourfold vision see,
> And a fourfold vision is given to me;
> 'Tis fourfold in my supreme delight
> And threefold in soft Beulah's night
> And twofold always. May God us keep
> From single vision & Newton's sleep!

His reference to "Newton's sleep" at the end here explicitly highlights his opposition to the rational and scientific perception of the world he felt that Newton embodied. In one of Blake's most famous visual images, he depicts a crouched Isaac Newton, holding a compass and gazing intently at a small scrap of paper, whilst ignorant of the beautiful colours and shapes of the organic forms growing on the rock behind him. When Blake wrote that "Wordsworth must know that what he writes Valuable is Not to be found in Nature", he meant that Wordsworth is guilty of the same mistake that Newton makes – that of accessing and admiring the material reality of the surrounding world, rather than transfiguring it into vision.

The divergences between Blake and Wordsworth regarding nature are quite usefully illuminated by consideration of one of Blake's more significant influences, Emanuel Swedenborg. Blake grew to disagree with many

Swedenborgian ideas, but there is no doubt the Swedish philosopher had a substantial influence on the *Songs*. Kathleen Raine, in *Blake and Tradition*, has expertly examined Blake's use of Swedenborgian symbolism. In particular, she highlights Swedenborg's concept of "influx", which she defines as follows:

> The world of nature and of man himself are but the lowest terms in a series of dependent spiritual causes. Natural forms and appearances of all kinds are the outward manifestation of a spiritual life and energy whose effect we see as the phenomena of nature. (Raine 4)

Complementing this influx is the idea of "correspondence", whereby everything within the natural world is inherently symbolic. This prioritising of the visionary truth behind the material reality of the world is at the heart of where Blake and Wordsworth differ. "Wordsworth," Raine writes, "found his symbols in nature – the image came first, a lesser celandine, a violet, a tree in a field – but Blake saw nature through symbol, not symbol through nature" (Raine 6). It is a visionary understanding of the world that Blake clearly and passionately articulates in *The Marriage of Heaven and Hell*, where he writes "A fool sees not the same tree that a wise man sees". As such – despite the surface similarities between the *Songs of Innocence and of Experience* and some of Wordsworth's lyrics – Blake and Wordsworth's perceptions of nature are in fact fundamentally opposed.

Ultimately, there are too many fundamental differences between Blake's work and the essential precepts of Romantic thought for the idea of Blake as a "Romantic poet" to be an acceptable definition. Peter Ackroyd identifies a variety of key differences between Blake and the Romantics, including Blake's dramatic approach to expression and the originality of his combination of words and visual images:

> These are often poems with an argumentative or satirical intent, and they are emphatically not expressions of lyrical feeling or the spontaneous overflowing of emotion in the conventional "romantic" mode ...

These are not poems as the "Lyrical Ballads" are poems: these are discrete works of art in which the words are only one element in a unified design.

As such, Ackroyd perceives Blake to be more appropriately situated, with regard to both his visual art and his poetry, within an eighteenth-century context of trade and public art rather than the withdrawn Romantic ideal into which he has so often been shoved: "His art is to be associated with Barry or Mortimer, not with Constable or Turner, just as he is better understood in the company of James Thomson or Edward Young rather than that of Wordsworth and Coleridge" (Ackroyd 73).

Even the shared political context of these writers, that of the French Revolution, brought about such divergent responses that it cannot usefully be understood as a point of connection between them. Blake was an urban poet, and a working poet, intimately involved in trade throughout his life; he would presumably have been appalled by Wordsworth and Coleridge's lofty withdrawal from commercial affairs. The difference between Wordsworth's rather remote attitude to the realities of urban life, and Blake's earthy confrontation of them, is underlined in "Composed Upon Westminster Bridge" and "London", two poems that present diametrically opposed visions of the same city at around the same time. Wordsworth's hopeful and celebratory sonnet represents an effort to purify London of all its industrial grime:

This City now doth like a garment wear
The beauty of the morning: silent, bare,
Ships, towers, domes, theatres, and temples lie
Open unto the fields, and to the sky,
All bright and glittering in the smokeless air.

This is a utopian vision of London, conveying nothing of its dirty reality as a living city. The harmony between the city's buildings, the surrounding fields, and the sky itself is absolute –

74

and as such, from a certain perspective, the poem is arguably one of Wordsworth's less successful pieces, despite its fame. This is certainly the case if we place value on a poem's honesty regarding the complexities and difficulties of human experience. Wordsworth sanitises London into a postcard of "smokeless" beauty, and in doing so nourishes a stereotypical image still occasionally attached to him, that of an aloof figure with little stomach for the grimy realities of urban life.

Blake's vision of the chartered streets, the blackening church, the harlot's curse, is not merely a contrasting vision of the city, but an embodiment of a fundamental difference between himself and Wordsworth: whilst the latter seeks harmony, Blake embraces conflict, confronting inequality and suffering whilst Wordsworth prefers to withdraw from it. Despite the continuing tendency for him to be linked with the Romantic tradition, Blake was no Romantic; Blake's work tends to sit uneasily with particular literary or artistic movements, and for many critics, the originality and strangeness of his visionary poetics ultimately resist placement within any particular tradition but his own.

# 11   Was Blake a Genius or a Madman?

William Blake, an unfortunate lunatic, whose personal
inoffensiveness secures him from confinement, and,
consequently, of whom no public notice would have
been taken, if he was not forced on the notice and
animadversion of the EXAMINER, in having been
held up to public admiration by many esteemed
amateurs and professors as a genius in some respect
original and legitimate ... Thus encouraged, the poor
man fancies himself a great master, and has painted a
few wretched pictures ... These he calls an Exhibition,
of which he has published a Catalogue, or rather a
farrago of nonsense, unintelligibleness, and egregious
vanity, the wild effusions of a distempered brain.

So wrote Robert Hunt, in an 1809 review of Blake's Broad
Street exhibition of his work. It was the only press review of
the exhibition; and perhaps unsurprisingly, its appearance
meant Blake never again held an exhibition throughout his
life, though he did occasionally exhibit works in galleries.
The review is evidence of a number of things, including the
struggle Blake had in his own lifetime to be fully accepted
and recognised as an artist and poet. It is also an early example of a view of Blake that has not entirely evaporated: that
of a mad, isolated figure, obsessively churning out artworks
from his "distempered brain" that indicate nothing so much
as his profound mental instability. The appearance of a 2007
*Daily Telegraph* feature on Blake, entitled "Loving Blake for
being bonkers", is an emphatic indication that the presentation of Blake as an unhinged literary loose cannon is far from
a thing of the past.

The idea of an overlap between genius and madness is
hardly uncommon, but few figures in literary history have

embodied this ambiguity quite so overtly as Blake, and it is one reason why he even now to some extent remains a divisive figure in narrative of English literature – his work simply too obscure, too idiosyncratic, for him to be accepted into some people's narrow conceptions of greatness or even artistic significance. Blake's own life was blighted by a persistent sense amongst other artists and writers that he was insane, and it was only towards the end of his life that unambiguous praise for his achievement starts to appear on record; Coleridge, for instance, wrote of Blake in 1818 that "He is a man of Genius – and I apprehend, a Swedenborgian – certainly, a mystic *emphatically*". Often, his work was greeted with a mixture of admiration and bafflement: Robert Southey called him a "painter of great but insane genius", and this double-edged response is characteristic of contemporary attitudes towards Blake's work. Wordsworth, too, concluded that "There is no doubt that this poor man was mad, but there is something in the madness of this man which interests me more than the Sanity of Lord Byron & Walter Scott." One of Blake's great friends and influences, Henry Fuseli, seems to have captured this ambivalence in a conversation with Joseph Farington, who reported Fuseli's views in his diary:

> Fuseli called on me last night & sat till 10 oClock. He mentioned Blake, the Engraver, whose genius & invention have been much spoken of. Fuseli has known him several years, and thinks He has a great deal of invention ... but the whole of his aim is to produce singular shapes & odd combinations ... Fuseli says, Blake has something of madness about him.

It is well-known that Blake experienced visions throughout his life, and these have often been cited as an example of his disturbed mental state. But what exactly were these visions, and what exactly did Blake see? He talked on many occasions of seeing angels, Biblical figures, dead relatives, and of having conversations with them as if they were as real as the living people around him. It seems clear that Blake experienced such visions as real, not as hallucinations or imagined experiences. John Beer writes that Blake "evidently enjoyed the power of eidetic vision, a condition in which human perception projects images so powerfully that the perceiver cannot easily tell the difference between them and images in the physical world" (Beer 5). These eidetic visions were an important component of his artistic vision, and they often fed themselves directly into his work. If anything, the frequency of his visions seems to have intensified as an adult, and at times interfered with his capacity for work. In 1802, he confessed to Thomas Butts that "I am not ashamed, afraid, or averse to tell you what Ought to be Told: That I am under the direction of Messengers from Heaven, Daily & Nightly". The reality of such visions, for Blake, explains a number of things, including his disdain for the straightforward nature-worship he saw in Wordsworth.

It is not, of course, simply Blake's visions that have accounted for his unbalanced reputation. From the outset, Blake found that the originality, the strangeness and the unparalleled ambition of his work led readers to resort to a decision that it was incoherent, absurd – "a farrago of nonsense", as Hunt put it. The nature of Blake's mythological constructions – the story of Orc and Los, Urizen, and the Four Zoas, which he tells in his long and often formidably difficult prophetic books – is single-handedly the most original and ambitious mythology in the history of English literature. Its intimidating complexity is combined with a commitment to such a radically visionary perception of the world that it is no surprise that rumours of madness still loom over him, despite that vast amount that has now been written about him and the nature of his achievement.

Ultimately, it is simply not a helpful line of consideration – since the integrity and power of the work remains, irrespective of any prurient speculations regarding the specifics of Blake's psychological stability. Blake has become one of the most profoundly influential writers over the last century, not just in literature and art but in popular culture too, casting a shadow over pop, rock, and folk music, film, new age culture, drugs, sport, and even (in 1997) the Queen's Christmas speech. His reputation as a writer, artist, and visionary is one of ever-increasing immensity of stature, immune to petty accusations of mental disturbance. While some might still side with Hunt's savage proposal that Blake's work constitutes the "wild effusions of a distempered brain", many more might incline towards the feelings of Peter Ackroyd, who in a recent television interview claimed that Blake was simply "the most powerful, the most significant philosopher or thinker in the course of English history."[1]

1 &lt;http://www.bbc.co.uk/news/av/entertainment-arts-17790481/five-minutes-with-peter-ackroyd&gt;

# Appendices

## (i) Blake and Drugs

Unlike various literary figures associated with the Romantic movement, there is no record of Blake ever taking drugs – and the very idea of it is somehow implausible, even absurd. Though it cannot be proved that he never did, we can take it as almost certain. The idea is fundamentally inconsistent with all accounts of the man and the nature of his relationship with the world. Blake did not require drugs of any kind, since transcendence was already all around him, in the form of his visions and astonishing imaginative power. It seems likely that Blake was a fairly abstemious man, rarely drinking and favouring a life of hard work in which pleasure-seeking was kept in its rightful place: "Fun I love", he once wrote, "but too much Fun is of all things the most loathsom [*sic*]."

It is therefore somewhat surprising that Blake has become perhaps the most powerful influence on drug consumption in the history of literature. The visionary nature of his writing has led various notable writers of succeeding generations to find versions of such visionary transcendence via mind-altering substances. In 1954, Aldous Huxley published *The Doors of Perception*, which describes his experiments with hallucinogenic drugs in an effort to achieve states of particular imaginative intensity. His title is taken from Blake's *The Marriage of Heaven and Hell*: "If the Doors of Perception were cleansed every thing would appear to man as it is, infinite". Huxley's work is, fundamentally, an effort to justify psychoactive drugs as an intellectually serious means of expanding one's horizons of mental perception. In it, he writes:

> To be shaken out of the ruts of ordinary perception, to be shown for a few timeless hours the outer and inner world, not as they appear to an animal obsessed with survival or to a human being obsessed with words and notions, but as they are apprehended, directly and unconditionally, by Mind at Large — this is an experience of inestimable value to everyone and especially to the intellectual.

Another writer to find narcotic inspiration in Blake is Allen Ginsberg, the American Beat poet. Blake was a serious influence on Ginsberg's work at a number of levels. Ginsberg based his innovative verse forms on a combination of Hebraic verse, Walt Whitman's poetry, and the long-line verses found in Blake's prophetic books. Blake also heavily influenced Ginsberg's anti-authoritarian spirituality – he developed Blake's proposition, "Every thing that lives is Holy", into a provocative and political expression of the same idea: "The world is holy! The soul is holy! The skin is holy! The nose is holy! The tongue and cock and hand and asshole holy!" (from "Footnote to *Howl*"). But Blake was also an inspirational presence with respect to Ginsberg's drug-induced visions. Aged twenty-six, Ginsberg heard the voice of Blake speaking to him in his apartment, and important connections can be traced between Blake's visionary understanding of the world and Ginsberg's well-documented use of psychoactive drugs in order to reach higher states of consciousness.

Similar connections can be made with numerous musicians, such as Jim Morrison and Julian Cope. Most recently, Pete Doherty's musical output – with the Libertines and with Babyshambles – has involved a much-hyped, much-maligned medley of upbeat melodies, drug-induced lyrical desolation and high-brow artistic and literary references, including the work and ideas of Blake.

# (ii)  Blake's Compositional Methods

Blake had been working as an engraver for seventeen years before producing any of his illuminated books. Apprenticed to James Basire in 1772, at the age of fourteen, Blake was trained in the conventional engraving methods of the time. Such work, whilst respectable, had serious limitations for those of deep artistic ambition, such as Blake – it mostly consisted of commissioned illustrations and engraving the works of other artists.

Blake later trained as an artist at the Royal Academy, but his illuminated printing method came as a significant breakthrough. John Thomas Smith, an early biographer of Blake, records that the idea arrived through a visitation from his beloved dead brother, Robert:

> Blake, after deeply perplexing himself as to the mode of accomplishing the publication of his illustrated songs, without their being subject to the expense of letter-press, his brother Robert stood before him in one of his visionary imaginations, and so decidedly directed him in the way in which he ought to proceed, that he immediately followed his advice, by writing his poetry, and drawing his marginal subjects of embellishments in outline upon the copper-plate with an impervious liquid, and then eating the plain parts or lights away with aquafortis considerably below them, so that the outlines were left as a stereotype. The plates in this state were then printed in any tint that he wished, to enable him or Mrs Blake to colour the marginal figures up by hand in imitation of drawings.

This method allowed Blake not only to continue the techniques of painting and engraving, but also to include both words and images in the same plate. Thus was born the techniques we see in evidence in the *Songs*, and which he went on to use in many of his later prophetic books.

Blake's new approach involved drawing everything – images, words, designs – in reverse on the plate. This skill of mirror writing, with its need for a reversed version of every text, might even be seen as influential in Blake's concept of contraries, and the importance he placed upon it. It requires no great stretch to see how the production of mirror writing – with its associations of doubling, of two simultaneously existing texts stretching in different directions, reflecting, and contradicting each other – might have significant underlying relevance to Blake's counterbalancing of "Innocence" and "Experience" and his idea that "Without contraries is no progression".

# (iii)  Blake's Mythology

One of the most intimidating elements of Blake for any reader is the astonishingly complex and extensive mythology he constructed and detailed in works such as *The Book of Thel*, *The Four Zoas*, *America*, *Europe*, *The Song of Los*, and *Jerusalem*. While the *Songs of Innocence and of Experience* can be read independently of this mythological system, it is – though often bewildering – highly useful in illuminating many of the key ideas Blake explores throughout his work. Some critics have argued that Blake articulated a coherent philosophy throughout his life, with his individual works forming interdependent parts of an overall tapestry of thought. From such a perspective, a thorough understanding of the details of his mythology is therefore a necessary bedrock to any full understanding of the *Songs*.

Some key figures in Blake's mythology are as follows:

### Albion

This was a traditional name for England, and it is with this meaning that Blake used the term in his earlier work. In his later prophetic books, however, Blake developed the figure of a giant named "Albion" who was both the father of all mankind and a personification of humanity's fallen state.

### Beulah

Meaning "married" or "bride" in Hebrew, the origin of this term is in the Old Testament, where is it used as a name for Palestine after the reunion of that land with God ("you will be called Hephzibah, and your land Beulah; for the Lord will take delight in you, and your land will be married", Isaiah 62:4). In Blake, Beulah is the realm of subconscious inspiration – of dreams, and of poetic inspiration. As such, Blake saw it as the fallen world in its very best condition – the closest mankind, in its fallenness, could get to an Edenic state. Its opposite is Ulro, the realm of physical matter, the darkest, most fallen state the world can reach.

### Four Zoas

These were the four beings Blake used to describe the fourfold division of all elements of humanity: their names were Los, Luvah, Tharmas, and Urizen. Blake seems to have taken the term "zoa" from the Book of Revelation, which describes four living creatures or beasts ("And one of the four beasts (*zoa*) gave unto the seven angels seven golden vials full of the wrath of God, who liveth for ever and ever", Revelation 15:7). If this is its origin, Blake treated the plural Greek word as if it were singular, turning it into the Anglicised plural "zoas".

### Har and Heva

Aged versions of Adam and Eve in a fallen world. They have three sons: Tiriel, Zazel, and Ijim. The story of Tiriel is told in Blake's unpublished poem of the same name.

### Los

One of the Four Zoas, Los represents the creative imagination.

*Luvah*

Another of the Four Zoas, Luvah represents passion and love.

*Tharmas*

Another of the Four Zoas, representing the senses and the physical body.

*Thel*

A figure of femininity whose story Blake tells in *The Book of Thel*. She is presented as an innocent girl on the verge of experience, afraid of motherhood, who questions a succession of symbolic figures – the Lily of the Valley, the Cloud, and the Clod of Clay with its Worm – about the nature and meaning of life.

*Urizen*

One of the Four Zoas, representing intellect and reason, but also associated with the Old Testament God, state religion, and kings. The name has variously been interpreted as a pun on "your reason", "horizon", and "orison". Urizen is especially important regarding Blake's perspective on Christianity. Blake associates Urizen with the God of the Fallen World, a God of restrictive laws and stifling reason – an oppressive ruler resembling the God worshipped by Christians, a God Blake perceived to be wrathful, totalitarian, and evil.

# (iv) The "Problem Songs"

Interpreting Blake's Songs is not made any easier by the fact that, in certain cases, Songs were switched in different editions from one collection to the other. How are we to read these particular poems? Should we side with the context of their original publication, or with the revised location to which Blake later moved them? The inescapable reality is that these Songs lurk on the borderlands of innocence and experience, representing neither one nor the other in any straightforward sense. A different kind of challenge is presented by those poems which do not appear in every edition of the *Songs* – raising questions about whether we should or should not include them in our consideration of the work.

### *"The Little Girl Lost" & "The Little Girl Found"*

This pair of poems was originally published in *Innocence*. Later, though – when Blake started to publish the *Songs* as a combined volume – they were almost invariably included in *Experience*. The subject matter, of Lyca's abandonment by her parents and subsequent capture by wild animals in a threatening, sexualised narrative – seems too dark for *Innocence*. Nowhere else, in that collection, is the loss of innocence described with such explicitness. Blake presumably felt that, despite Lyca's ultimate reunion with her parents, the subject matter of sexual self-discovery was more in tune with *Experience*, hence the change.

*"The Voice of the Ancient Bard"*

This was originally published in *Innocence*, but shifted to *Experience* in the combined editions Blake published towards the end of his life. The poem, addressing the "Youth of delight", optimistically describes an "opening morn" that suggests forthcoming hope and possibility. But it also details the victims of "Folly", who "wish to lead others when they should be led": this may be a commentary on the adult figures of experience and their efforts to "lead", and restrict, childhood freedoms. The fact that the voice of the poem is that of the "Bard", not a poet or piper, suggests proximity to experience: engraved in a different script to the other *Innocence* songs, it was probably the last of them to be written.

*"To Tirzah"*

This poem did not appear in original editions of *Experience*, but was added to later copies. Tirzah was one of the daughters of Zelophehad in the Old Testament. Blake uses her in this poem to represent the physical body ("Thou mother of my Mortal part"), which the poet rejects in an effort to assert the spirituality within man's physical nature ("The death of Jesus set me free,/ Then what have I to do with thee?").

*"A Divine Image"*

The contrary of this Song in *Innocence* ("The Divine Image") presents a harmonious picture of God's love and forgiveness, expressing Blake's belief that these divine qualities actually reside in mankind:

> For Mercy, Pity, Peace, and Love
> Is God, our father dear,
> And Mercy, Pity, Peace, and Love
> Is Man, his child and care.

In contrast, "A Divine Image" bleakly presents humanity as corrupt, cruel, and dishonest:

> Cruelty has a human heart,
> And Jealousy a human face;
> Terror the human form divine,
> And secrecy the human dress.

The question of whether to include this in the *Songs* at all, though, is rather complicated – it was only ever included in one copy produced in Blake's lifetime.

## (v) What Were Blake's Visions?

The first may have happened when he was just four. "You know, dear," his wife once reminded him, "the first time you saw God was when you were four years old. And he put his head to the window and set you ascreaming." The visions did not always make Blake's childhood easy: on one occasion, his father threatened to beat him for claiming that he had just seen the prophet Ezekiel under a tree.

These visions imbued Blake with a powerful sense of the immediate presence of the spiritual realm. The most likely scientific explanation for them is that they were a form of eidetic imagery – what we commonly call "photographic memory", the ability to recall memories and images with as much clarity as direct sensory perceptions. It seems probable that this is the condition Blake either suffered from, or was blessed with – interpreting it throughout his life as proof that the physical and spiritual are not segregated dimensions, but are in unity with each other. It was a belief encouraged by Blake's reading of Emanuel Swedenborg, who claimed in his writings that "I have spoken with many spirits ... it has been my destiny to live for years in company with spirits ... I have conversed about this with the angels."

Blake is famous for these visions, and they have often been used as fuel to support the idea of his supposed "madness". What is less well-documented is that reports of such visions were not especially uncommon in eighteenth-century England: numerous other prominent figures of the time seemed to have experienced something similar. According to David Erdman, "Hogarth, scarcely a mystic, saw visions; and many other artists, including Cosway, who taught at Pars's Drawing School and was intimate with Blake for many years, boasted of ghostly visitors who sat for their portraits."

## (vi)  Musicians Inspired by Blake

### Hubert Parry

Perhaps the most famous musical adaptation of Blake is Hubert Parry's rousing version of "Jerusalem", composed in 1916. The lyric actually appears as part of a Preface to Blake's long poem, *Milton*: the title "Jerusalem" was Parry's addition.

### Benjamin Britten

Britten seems to have been preoccupied with Blake's work, adapting parts of it on several different occasions. In his 1943 work, *Songs for Tenor, Horn and Strings*, he created a setting of "The Sick Rose"; in 1965, he incorporated a range of Blake material into *Songs and Proverbs of William Blake*.

### Jim Morrison

The Doors took their name from a line in Blake's *The Marriage of Heaven and Hell*: "If the Doors of Perception were cleansed every thing would appear to man as it is, infinite". Jim Morrison encountered Blake through Aldous Huxley, and his 1954 work *The Doors of Perception*.

### Van Morrison

In "Let the Slave", a song from Van Morrison's 1998 album *A Sense of Wonder*, he uses lines from Blake's *Vala, or The Four Zoas*:

Let the slave, grinding at the mill, run out into the field;
Let him look up into the heavens & laugh in the bright air.
Let the inchained soul, shut up in darkness & in sighing
Whose face has never seen a smile in thirty weary years,
Rise & look out: his chains are loose, his dungeon doors are open;
And let his wife & children return from the oppressor's scourge.

## William Bolcom

The most extensive and ambitious musical adaptation of Blake ever attempted is perhaps Bolcom's *Songs of Innocence and of Experience*, a three-hour orchestral piece which he composed over a period of twenty-five years between 1956 and 1981.

## Jah Wobble

Wobble's 2000 album *The Inspiration of William Blake* is rich with Blake allusions and references. "Blake was nonconformist and imaginative and rule-breaking", said Wobble in a 2009 interview. "If Blake had been my age in the 1970s, he would have been on the punk scene, without a doubt. He was a regular London bloke who worked for a living."

## Patti Smith

Smith has highlighted her debt to William Blake in a number of interviews. In a 2004 Rolling Stone interview, she commented: "I was reading William Blake as a child. *Songs of Innocence* was next to Winnie the Pooh and Black Beauty. And I learned things – about chimney sweeps and the terrible child labor [*sic*] of his time. I could see he cared about children. The second way I came to Blake was as a painter:

I studied his work and palette. More recently, I've studied Blake the man. And what I learned was that this was a man who had visions as a child, who was ridiculed and even beaten for having these visions. But he maintained those visions his whole life. Wherever they came from, whether he animated them from within or they were from God, William Blake held on to his vision. He never got a break in his life. His work never sold. He lived in poverty. When he spoke out, he nearly lost his life. He could have been hanged for insurrection."

*Bruce Dickinson*

Iron Maiden frontman Dickinson released a solo album, *The Chemical Wedding*, in 1998 which was largely inspired by Blake. The album features songs such as "Book of Thel", "Gates of Urizen", and "Jerusalem", and includes various spoken and sung excerpts from Blake's work.

*Ulver*

The most extreme group to have been inspired by Blake might be Ulver, a Norwegian black metal band. In 1999, they released *Themes from William Blake's The Marriage of Heaven & Hell*. According to their frontman Kristoffer Rygg (known as "Garm"), "With that album we were obviously revolting against what we saw as totally narrow-minded rhetoric and cheap gimmicks coming from our contemporaries. Blake did the same in his time – not by simple negation, but by refining and/or challenging the perceptions and preconceptions of his fellowmen."

*Richard Ashcroft*

"History", a song from The Verve's 1995 debut album *A Northern Soul*, is partly inspired by "London" from the *Songs of Experience*. Ashcroft's opening lyrics in the song closely resemble the opening lines of Blake's poem.

*Pete Doherty*

Blake's work has been one of Doherty's key sources of inspiration throughout his troubled career (a bright student, Doherty was himself a prize-winning poet as a teenager). In 2005, Doherty's band Babyshambles released their debut album entitled *Down in Albion*, which describes a nostalgic and idealised vision of ancient England based, in part, on Blake's (rather different) concept of Albion.

*Testament*

Hip-hop artist Testament put on a Blake-inspired show, *Blake Remixed*, in 2015. "I might be stretching it," he commented, "but I believe if William Blake were alive he would be a hip-hop rapper."

## (vii)  Blake on His Own Work

"I find more & more that my Style of designing is a Species by itself, & in this which I send you have been compell'd by my Genius or Angel to follow where he led; if I were to act otherwise it would not fulfill the purpose for which alone I live, which is ... to renew the lost Art of the Greeks."

– From a letter to John Trusler, 16 August 1799.

"But I am happy to find a great Majority of Fellow Mortals who can Elucidate My Visions, & Particularly they have been Elucidated by Children, who have taken a greater delight in contemplating my Pictures than I even hoped. Neither Youth nor Childhood is Folly or Incapacity. Some Children are Fools & so are some Old Men. But There is a vast majority on the side of Imagination or Spiritual Sensation."

– From a letter to John Trusler, 23 August 1799.

"I live by Miracle. I am Painting small Pictures from the Bible. For as to Engraving, in which art I cannot reproach myself with any neglect, yet I am laid by in a corner as if I did not Exist, & since my Young's Night Thoughts have been publish'd, Even Johnson & Fuseli have discarded my Graver. But as I know that He who Works & has his health cannot starve, I laugh at Fortune & Go on & on."

– From a letter to George Cumberland, 26 August 1799.

"I know myself both Poet & Painter."

– From a letter to Thomas Butts, 6 July 1803.

"Yet I laugh & sing, for if on Earth neglected I am in heaven a Prince among Princes, & even on Earth beloved by the Good as a Good Man; this I should be perfectly contented with, but at certain periods a blaze of reputation arises round me in which I am consider'd as one distinguish'd by some mental perfection, but the flame soon dies again & I am left stupefied and astonish'd."

– From a letter to William Hayley, 7 October 1803.

## (viii)  Ten Facts About William Blake

1.  In the summer of 1803, Blake was accused of sedition. Despite Blake's subversive political attitudes, the circumstances of this particular affair were mundane, even bizarre. Blake had turned a soldier, John Scofield, out of his garden; Scofield, taking exception to this, accused Blake of making various remarks against the King. In such unstable times, when the English authorities were paranoid about the possibility of an uprising like those in America and France, it was enough to bring Blake to trial. Scofield, though, had no witnesses to support his story; Blake was acquitted in January 1804.

2.  One of the more popular stories about Blake and his eccentric ways is that he and his wife were once discovered naked in their garden, reciting passages from *Paradise Lost*. The story comes from Thomas Butts, who was Blake's patron for many years. Critics and biographers disagree on the reliability of this anecdote, but Peter Ackroyd suggests that the respectable gentleman Butts "is highly unlikely to have invented the story", and that dismissive critics have simply not understood "the religious radicalism with which Blake was at least marginally involved" (Ackroyd 157).

3.  "The Tyger" remains probably the most anthologised English poem. Such a title is a matter of debate, since reliable statistics in this area are hard to come by. But many critics writing on Blake support the idea. Robert Essick, for instance, suggests that "The Tyger" is not simply Blake's "most famous poem", but "probably the most frequently anthologised poem in English" (Essick 115).

4.  Blake was especially close to his youngest brother, Robert, whose death at the age of nineteen left him distraught. For the rest of Blake's life, he saw Robert in visions. According to a contemporary account, in one such vision Robert

revealed to him the new method he could use in order to engrave his recently completed *Songs of Innocence*: "Blake, after deeply perplexing himself as to the mode of accomplishing the publication of his illustrated songs without their being subject to the expense of a letter-press, his brother Robert stood before him in one of his visionary imaginations, and so decidedly directed him in the way in which he ought to proceed, that he immediately followed his advice".

5. Blake struggled throughout his life to get his work accepted by the artistic authorities of the time. In his advertisement for his 1809 exhibition of paintings, he wrote: "The execution of my Designs, being all in Water-colours, (that is in Fresco) are regularly refused to be exhibited by the *Royal Academy*, and the *British Institution* has, this year, followed its example, and has effectually excluded me by this Resolution; I therefore invite those Noblemen and Gentlemen, who are its Subscribers, to inspect what they have excluded: and those who have been told that my Works are but an unscientific and irregular Eccentricity, a Madman's Scrawls, I demand of them to do me the justice to examine before they decide."

6. Throughout his life, Blake's fortunes were inconsistent: his poetic works generally sold very little, and he found unreliable income from commissioned engravings. In the latter part of his life, he descended into poverty and isolation. In 1815, in order to make ends meet, he was forced to accept a commission to engrave images on pieces of crockery – teapots, egg cups, and soup tureens – from the factory of Josiah Wedgwood, a prosperous tradesman and potter.

7. Blake died in his home at 3 Fountain Court on 12 August, 1827. A friend, George Richmond, claimed to have been with Blake and his wife at the moment of death, and wrote: "He died on Sunday night at 6 oClock in a most glorious

manner. He said He was going to that Country he had all His life wished to see & expressed Himself Happy, hoping for Salvation through Jesus Christ – Just before he died His Countenance became fair. His eyes Brighten'd and He burst out into Singing of the things he saw in Heaven."

8. There are popular rumours about Blake's "lost works". Blake's own comment that he had written "Six or Seven Epic poems as long as Homer and 20 Tragedies as long as Macbeth" perhaps supports the idea that there must be various works that remain undiscovered. One theory is that Frederick Tatham, who wrote the first biography of Blake, inherited various manuscripts from Catherine which he burned, believing them to be blasphemous and heretical.

9. In 1997, the year in which Princess Diana died, Blake made an appearance in the Queen's Christmas speech. Quoting from Blake's "Auguries of Innocence", she said: "Joy and sadness are part of all our lives. Indeed, the poet William Blake tells us that 'Joy and woe are woven fine,/A clothing for the soul divine,/Under every grief and pine/Runs a joy with silken twine.' The interweaving of joy and woe has been very much brought home to me and my family during the last months. We all felt the shock and sorrow of Diana's death."

10. Blake remains a key inspiration for many contemporary writers. Phillip Pullman worked aspects of Blake's ideas into his enormously popular and successful trilogy, *His Dark Materials*. Each chapter from the final novel in the sequence, *The Amber Spyglass*, begins with a quotation from Blake. Pullman is also President of the William Blake Society.

# (ix)  Blake on Film

Mean Streets, *dir. Martin Scorsese (1973)*

In one scene from this movie, the character Tony (played by David Proval) reveals he has acquired two pet tigers. "I really wanted to get a tiger, Charlie", he confesses as he enters the cage to feed them and the others take refuge on top of a sofa. "Ol' William Blake and all that." The animals, symbolising the menace and threat of 1970s New York, represent an intriguing allusion to Blake's "The Tyger".

Blade Runner, *dir. Ridley Scott (1982)*

Roy Batty (played by Rutger Hauer), the villainous replicant antagonist in Ridley Scott's science-fiction masterpiece, makes reference to Blake when he enters the eye manufacturing plant, Eye World: "Fiery the angels fell; deep thunder rode around their shores, burning with the fires of Orc." Hauer himself included these lines, which were not originally in the script. They are a deliberate misquotation of lines from Blake's *America: A Prophecy*:

> Fiery the Angels rose, & as they rose deep thunder roll'd
> Around their shores, indignant burning with the fires of Orc;

Hauer's substitution of "angels fell" rather than "angels rose" highlights the idea that the replicants are fallen angels, and supports the idea – suggested elsewhere on the film – of Roy as a version of Lucifer (though he also displays Christ-like characteristics towards the film's end).

Dead Man, *dir. Jim Jarmusch (1995)*

In this intriguing postmodern Western, Johnny Depp plays a character named William Blake, who is claimed by another character to be the reincarnation of Blake the poet. Various allusions to Blake's work are weaved into the film. On his use of Blake, Jarmusch said:

> I collected all my notes on the film and was about to write the script and I was reading all these books by American Indian people. Then I put all that stuff away and picked up William Blake, who I read a lot when I was younger but hadn't read for a while, and I was just struck by the connection in thought between a lot of the stuff I was reading and a lot of Blake's work. He just walked into the film on his own. After the film was shot, I started seeing even more connections. If you're interested in Blake, it's woven in there pretty deeply.

Red Dragon, *dir. Brett Ratner (2002)*

In this adaptation of Thomas Harris' novel, serial killer Francis Dolarhyde is obsessed with Blake's painting, *The Great Red Dragon and the Woman Clothed in the Sun*. One scene features Dolarhyde finding this painting in the Brooklyn Museum, tearing it to pieces, and eating it.

# Bibliography

Ackroyd, Peter, *Blake*, Sinclair Stevenson, 1995.

Barthes, Roland, *Image-Music-Text*, trans. Stephen Heath, Fontana, 1977.

Beer, John, *William Blake: A Literary Life*, Palgrave Macmillan, 2007.

Behrendt, Stephen, "The 'Third Text' of Blake's Illuminated Books", in *Blake's Poetry and Designs*, ed. Johnson and Grant.

Bruder, Helen P., *William Blake and the Daughters of Albion*, Macmillan, 1997.

Eaves, Morris, "Introduction: to paradise the hard way", in *The Cambridge Companion to William Blake*, ed. Morris Eaves.

Eaves, Morris, ed., *The Cambridge Companion to William Blake*, Cambridge University Press, 2003.

Erdman, David, *Blake: Prophet Against Empire*, 3rd edn, Princeton University Press, 1977.

Erdman, David, ed., *The Complete Poetry & Prose of William Blake*, Random House, 1988.

Essick, Robert, ed., *Songs of Innocence and of Experience*, Huntingdon Library, 2008.

Ferber, Michael, *The Poetry of William Blake*, Penguin, 1991.

Foster Damon, S., *A Blake Dictionary: The Ideas and Symbols of William Blake*, University Press of New England, 1988.

Frye, Northrop, *Fearful Symmetry: A Study of William Blake*, Princeton University Press, 1947.

Gardner, Stanley, *Blake*, Evans Bros, 1968.

Gardner, Stanley, *The Tyger The Lamb and the Terrible Desart: Songs of Innocence and of Experience in its times and circumstance*, Cygnus Arts, 1998.

Glen, Heather, *Vision and Disenchantment: Blake's Songs & Wordsworth's Lyrical Ballads*, Cambridge University Press, 1983.

Hilton, Nelson, "Blake's Early Works", in *The Cambridge Companion to William Blake*, ed. Morris Eaves.

Johnson, Mary Lynn and Grant, John E., eds, *Blake's Poetry and Designs*, Norton, 2008.

Keynes, Geoffrey, ed., *Blake: Complete Writings*, Oxford University Press, 1966.

Leader, Zachary, *Reading Blake's Songs*, Routledge, 1981.

Makdisi, Saree, *Reading William Blake*, Cambridge University Press, 2015.

Maxwell, Glyn, *On Poetry*, Harvard University Press, 2013.

Pound, Ezra, *ABC of Reading*, New Directions Paperback, 2010.

Punter, David, *New Casebooks: William Blake*, Macmillan, 1996.

Raine, Kathleen, *Blake and Tradition*, Princeton University Press, 1968.

Roberts, Jonathan, *William Blake's Poetry: A Reader's Guide*, Continuum, 2007.

Ryan, Robert, "Blake and Religion", in *The Cambridge Companion to William Blake*, ed. Morris Eaves.

Simpson, David, "Blake and Romanticism", in *The Cambridge Companion to William Blake*, ed. Morris Eaves.

Stevenson, W. H., *Blake: The Complete Poems*, Pearson, 2007.

William Blake Archive website: <http://www.blakearchive.org>.

Willmott, Richard, ed., *William Blake: Songs of Innocence and of Experience*, Oxford University Press, 2011.

Wolfson, Susan J., "Blake's language in poetic form", in *The Cambridge Companion to William Blake*, ed. Morris Eaves.

# Index

The All Blacks have spent a record 743 total weeks at the top of the IRB World Rankings

---

Rugby is named after Rugby School, the school attended by rugby's inventor William Webb Ellis

---

21 players have won the Rugby World Cup twice, no one has won it three times

---

The top division of rugby in France is the Top 14

---

Wales legend Neil Jenkins scored 263 points in 1999, the most any player has scored in a calendar year of international rugby

Rugby Union became a professional sport in 1995

---

Four All Blacks coaches have achieved 100% win records during their time in charge of New Zealand

---

England's 38-38 draw with Scotland in the 2019 Six Nations is the highest-scoring draw in the history of the competition

---

Both South Africa and New Zealand have won a record three World Cups

---

Super Rugby is the name of the league that contains clubs from Australia, Fiji, New Zealand and the Pacific Islands, it once contained Argentine, Japanese and South African clubs too

Italy were added to the Five Nations in 2000, making it the Six Nations as we know it today

Argentina joined the Tri-Nations in 2012, to form the Rugby Championship

The first Rugby World Cup was held in 1987, it was hosted and won by New Zealand

Eddie Jones has a better win percentage as England Manager than any other coach in their history, including Sir Clive Woodward

Wallabies skipper Michael Hooper is the only player in history to have received nine yellow cards in international rugby

Until 1977, tries were only worth three points, they were then initially raised to four

---

Dan Carter has scored more points in international rugby than any other player, he scored 1598 points in his 112 caps for the All Blacks

---

The 2015 Rugby World Cup was the highest-attended Rugby World Cup in history, with 2,477,805 fans attending matches

---

Scotland won the first game of rugby ever played, they beat England 1-0, converting a try

---

Richie McCaw is the most capped All Black in history, he made 148 appearances for New Zealand, winning two World Cups

Twickenham is the world's largest rugby stadium, which can seat 82,000 fans

Springbok winger Bryan Habana once had a race with a Cheetah

Ben Youngs became England's most-capped player in history in 2022, he overtook legendary prop Jason Leonard

Scotland's Ian Smith is the only player to have scored three hat tricks in Six Nations history, he achieved these in 1924 and 1925

Both of the French players that have won the World Rugby Player of the Year award were scrum-half, Fabien Galthie in 2002, and Antoine Dupont in 2021

The Ancient Romans played a similar game to rugby 2000 years ago, known as 'Harpastum'

Ireland's Tony O'Reilly is the British and Irish Lions' top try scorer in history, he scored six tries in the 1955 and 1959 tours

New Zealand's 145-17 thrashing of Japan at the 1995 World Cup is the highest-scoring World Cup match in history

Argentina were ranked as the world's third-best side in 2007 and 2008

England fans sing 'Swing Low Sweet Chariot' to support their team

The first game of international rugby was played in 1871, a year before the first game of football was played, both matches were England v. Scotland

---

Only four countries have won the Rugby World Cup: New Zealand, South Africa, Australia and England

---

Rugby was invented sixty years before American Football

---

Steve Hansen managed the All Blacks for a record 107 tests, before retiring in 2019

---

The Oxford Dictionary first mentioned the game of rugby in 1852

No Northern Hemisphere side got past the quarter-finals of the 2015 Rugby World Cup

France, New Zealand and Australia are the only three teams to have reached the quarter-finals of every World Cup tournament

In 2012, England's Manu Tuilagi broke the tackles of All Blacks legends Dan Carter, Richie McCaw and Aaron Smith, before passing the ball to Chris Ashton to score

Japan's highest world ranking is seventh, they achieved this in 2019

The 2019 Rugby World Cup tournament saw the first cancellation of matches in Rugby World Cup history with Typhoon Hagibis cancelling three matches due to the impact on safety that it would have had

The British and Irish Lions have not won a tour since they travelled to Australia in 2013

---

In 1888 the New Zealand Native team toured Great Britain and Ireland and performed the Haka before their matches for the first time in history

---

Rugby Union was an Olympic sport, it featured in 1900, 1908, 1920, and 1924

---

Gordon D'Arcy won the first Six Nations Championship Player of the Championship award, which was awarded in 2004

---

When Jonny Wilkinson scored the drop goal, to put England 20-17 up against Australia in the 2003 World Cup Final, there were just 26 seconds left of extra-time

The first Women's World Cup was played in 1991 and was won by the USA

---

A Six Nations Grand Slam is when one team wins all of their matches

---

Argentina have won the Wooden Spoon in the Rugby Championship every year since joining in 2012, aside from 2015, when South Africa finished bottom

---

The Rugby World Cup is held every four years, just like the FIFA World Cup and the Olympics

---

No player has ever won Women's Player of the Year twice

In the 2019 World Cup, South Africa became the first team to win the World Cup after losing a group stage match, they lost to the All Blacks in the groups 23-13

In England, there are 2,099 registered rugby clubs

Richie McCaw and Dan Carter have both won three World Rugby Player of the Year awards, more than any other player

In 1995 Nelson Mandela, the President of South Africa, historically wore a Springboks rugby shirt and cap to present the Webb Ellis Cup to the South African captain Francois Pienaar

New Zealand achieved the highest-ever IRB rating points, they reached 96.57 points out of 100 in 2016

Japan is the only Asian nation that has reached the World Cup knockout stages

Rugby is currently the fastest-growing sport in the USA

Jonny Wilkinson and Owen Farrell are the only two England players to have ever scored over 1000 points in international rugby

American Samoa are the lowest-ranked team in World Rugby, they sit at 109 in the IRB World Rankings

Richie McCaw scored four tries in three matches against Italy

Crusaders Prop Wyatt Crockett has made the most Super Rugby appearances in history

Sergio Parisse has played a record 69 matches in the Six Nations

The 'Wooden Spoon' is awarded to the team that finishes bottom of the Six Nations

In a 2006 test match between Wales and New Zealand, the All Blacks performed the Haka in the changing room before the match, after Wales requested to sing 'Hen Wlad Fy Nhadau' after the Haka was performed on the pitch, as they had done in 1905

Rugby passes can go backwards or flat, but of course, cannot go forward

England's Women have reached the World Cup Final at every tournament apart from the 1998 World Cup, they finished third in this tournament

---

Argentina dropped out of the top 10 in the World Rankings for the first time in 2014

---

Nearly seven million people worldwide are registered to play for a rugby team

---

Leinster are the most successful team in the United Rugby Championship history, with 8 titles

---

The most famous of New Zealand's Hakas is called "Ka Mate", and was believed to be first performed by the All Blacks in 1905

Numbers 1-8 are worn by forwards, numbers 9-15 are worn by backs

Wales sang their national anthem in 1905 when Wales faced New Zealand, this is believed to be the first sporting occasion in which a national anthem was sung before ever

Scotland play their home matches at Murrayfield

Jonny Wilkinson is the only English player that has ever won the World Rugby Player of the Year award

New Zealand spent ten years at the top of the IRB World Rankings, from 2009-2019

Membership to play for the Barbarians is invitational only

---

Jonah Lomu scored four tries against England in the semi-final of the 1995 World Cup, no player has scored this many tries since in that stage of the competition

---

France have faced England more than any other nation in their history, but have only won around 38% of their games against England

---

Emily Scarratt scored 44 points in the 2021 Women's Rugby World Cup, the most of any player

---

The first ever club rugby match in history took place between Richmond and Blackheath in 1863, 8 years before the first international match would take place

Richie McCaw was the cover star of the Rugby 08 video game

Brian O'Driscoll is the top try scorer in international rugby history for a non-winger, the Irish centre scored 47 times in 141 caps for Ireland

Springbok coach Rassie Erasmus has released clips on social media, breaking down his issues with refereeing, the video he produced after the Lions tour earned him a two-month ban from World Rugby

Saracens won back-to-back European Rugby Champions Cups in 2016 and 2017, winning again in 2019

Stuart Hogg became Scotland's all-time top try scorer with a try against Japan in 2021

A kick along the floor in rugby is referred to as a 'grubber' kick

---

Saracens Women's have won three of the four Premier 15s Finals

---

As of 2022, Wales have won exactly half of the 102 matches they have played against France

---

There were no tries scored in the 1995 World Cup Final, but three drop goals were scored, including a winning drop goal from South Africa's Joel Stransky

---

Stade Toulousain have won the Top 14 title a record 21 times

According to the Guinness Book of Records, 64.22m is the longest-scored place kick in rugby history, it was completed by Paul Thorburn in 1986 for Wales

Irish players have won the Six Nations Player of the Championship the most times in history

Richie McCaw won the New Zealand Sportsman of the Decade Award, this is the highest award any sportsperson from New Zealand can be awarded

Irish teams are the most successful in the history of the United Rugby Championship, they have won 13 titles

Over 857 million people tuned in to watch the 2019 Rugby World Cup

Argentine club side Jaguares reached the final of the 2019 Super Rugby, making them the only team from Argentina to ever achieve that feat, but they lost 19-3 to the Crusaders

---

Offside is the most common reason for penalties to be awarded in rugby

---

Jonny Wilkinson's drop goal to win the 2003 World Cup was on his weaker right foot and it was his third attempt at a drop goal of the day

---

New Zealand would have to wait for five tournaments to win their second World Cup, after winning the first World Cup in 1987, they didn't win again until 2011

---

The first Pacific Tri-Nations competition, between Tonga, Fiji and Samoa was held in 1982 with Samoa winning the first cup, it was replaced by the Pacific Nations Cup in 2006

In 2015, South Africa finished bottom of the Rugby Championship, just four years later they won the World Cup

---

Australian fly-half Quade Cooper received three yellow cards in 2015 for Australia, he only played five matches that year and earned two of them coming on as a replacement

---

Five nations hosted the 1991 World Cup: England, France, Ireland, Wales and Scotland

---

Argentina have reached the Rugby World Cup Semi-Final twice, even finishing third in the competition in 2007

---

English players have won Women's World Rugby Player of the Year the most times, with eight victories for English players

The legend goes that Harlequins were named as such as their team looked through a dictionary to find a word they all found funny and interesting, and they all agreed on Harlequins

---

Two-thirds of the All Blacks team were struck with food poisoning the night before the 1995 World Cup Final, they would lose the following day 15-12 to South Africa, despite being heavy favourites to win the cup

---

Scotland wore a brown kit for the first-ever rugby match in history, England wore a white kit

---

The British and Irish Lions lost 3-0 in their 2005 tour to New Zealand

---

Play-offs were introduced into Premiership Rugby in 2002

Spain reached their highest ranking in rugby history in 2022, they rose to 15th on the IRB World Rankings

---

Clermont Auvergne have won the Top 14 title twice, but have been runners-up a record 12 times

---

The 1961 All Blacks vs France match was played in near hurricane conditions, the wind was so strong that the French kicker cleared the ball from his own 22-metre line, only for it to blow back behind him and out past own dead ball line

---

New Zealand have won the Wooden Spoon twice in the history of the Rugby Championship in 1998 and 2004

---

A 'tap-tackle' is performed when a player taps the ankle or foot of their opponent, typically as a last-ditch attempt, the tap usually buckles the attacking player, causing them to fall over

No player that has won the World Rugby Junior Player of the Year has ever gone on to win the World Rugby Player of the Year award

---

Early scrums only had two players in the front row, with three in the second row behind them, it wasn't until the 1920s that this changed

---

All Black winger Joe Rokocoko score 17 tries in 12 matches in 2003, the most any player has scored in a calendar year of international rugby

---

In total, 15 matches are played in each Six Nations competition

---

In seven meetings, Wales have beaten the USA seven times and scored 305 points against the Eagles

London Wasps won the first three rugby Premiership Finals, beating Gloucester, Bath and then Leicester

---

Bryan Habana is the top try scorer in Rugby Championship history, with 21 tries for the Springboks

---

Maro Itoje won the 2016 World Rugby Breakthrough Player of the Year award

---

The Barbarians have defeated the All Blacks twice, lost eight times and drawn once

---

England were fined £2000 following the 2019 Rugby World Cup Semi-Final as they formed a V-Shape in opposition to the Haka

Harlequins won the 2021 Premiership after finishing fourth in the table during the regular season

---

The Junior All Blacks won the first two Pacific Nations Cup titles

---

In 1951, Puma winger Uriel O'Farrell scored seven tries in a match against Uruguay, no one has ever managed to score seven tries in a test match since

---

Toulon have played in four Challenge Cup Finals, without ever winning the title

---

Five points for a try only became an active rule in rugby in 1992

Seattle Seawolves are America's most successful club rugby side

---

Toulouse have won a record five European Rugby Champions Cups

---

Once a player has lost their original bind in a maul, they can only rejoin the maul from the back

---

Rugby first featured at the 1900 Olympic games, nowadays we have Rugby 7s as part of the Olympics

---

In 2001, England beat Romania 134-0, their biggest victory of all time, Dan Luger, Ben Cohen and Jason Robinson all scored hat tricks and Charlie Hodgson converted 14 tries

New Zealand and England are the only two teams that have recorded 18 consecutive wins in test matches, Ireland ended both of these winning streaks

---

In 2012, Manu Tuilagi intercepted an All Blacks pass, and ran in from the halfway line before holding up the 'Loser' sign on his forehead to the New Zealand team

---

William Webb Ellis was the first inductee of the World Rugby Hall of Fame

---

Mike Brown is the only English player to have ever won the Six Nations Championship Player of the Championship award

---

Chris Robshaw is the only player to have ever won the Premiership Player of the Year award twice

Former Ireland fly-half Ronan O'Gara led La Rochelle to back-to-back Champions Cup Finals, winning the title in 2022 with a tight 24-21 win against Leinster

---

Ten of the sixteen winners of the World Rugby Player of the Year award have been All Blacks players

---

Argentina's 48-17 win over Australia in the 2022 Rugby Championship was their biggest-ever win against the Wallabies

---

England, New Zealand, South Africa and Australia have never dropped out of the top 10 IRB World Rankings

---

France are second on the list of most points scored of all-time, behind the All Blacks

Saracens won their first Premiership Final in 2011, they beat Leicester 22-18

Wales played their first international match ten years after Scotland and England faced off for the first time

Rory Underwood is England's all-time top try scorer, he scored 49 tries for England

The United Hospitals Challenge Cup was the first rugby competition in history, it was founded in 1874 and won by Guy's Hospital

England have only ever lost twice in matches where Antony Watson has scored a try

Jonny Wilkinson is the World Cup's all-time top point scorer, he scored 277 at four World Cup tournaments

---

In 2022, South Africa recorded back-to-back wins against the All Blacks, they hadn't achieved this for 13 years

---

Field goals were abolished in 1905 from Rugby Union

---

Thibaut Privat made 387 Top 14 appearances for five different clubs, making him the player with the most appearances in the competition's history

---

England's 2003 World Cup win against Australia was played in Sydney

Sonny Bill Williams was sent off for a shoulder charge to the head of Anthony Watson in the second test of the 2017 British and Irish Lions tour

---

The 2031 Rugby World Cup will be hosted by the USA for the first time

---

All Blacks teammates Richie Mo'Unga and Beauden Barrett faced each other in the 2022 Super Rugby Final, Mo'Unga and the Crusaders came out on top on that occasion

---

Cyril Low and Ian Smith have both scored eight tries in a single Six Nations Championship, more than any other player has managed

---

The same pair of nations have faced each other in two separate World Cup Finals on three occasions: France and New Zealand in 1987 and 2011, Australia and England in 1991 and 2003, and South Africa and England in 2007 and 2019

England have a winning record against every team they have ever faced, aside from New Zealand and South Africa

---

The winning penalty kick in the 2011 Rugby World Cup was taken by Stephen Donald, who was the All Blacks fifth choice kicker

---

Cadbury's chocolate is currently the official Sponsor of Australia Rugby

---

Fly-halves have won the most World Rugby Player of the Year awards, with seven awards to date, Flanker's have won five awards and are in second place

---

Angus Buchanan was the first man in history to score an international try

The closest final in the history of Premiership rugby took place in the 2008-09 season, Leicester beat London Irish 10-9

New Zealand 8-7 France was the closest World Cup Final result in history, it occurred in 2011

Exeter Chiefs won their first European Rugby Champions Cup in 2020, beating Racing 92 by just four points in the final

Indonesia's rugby team are known as the 'White Rhinos'

England's last Six Nations Grand Slam win was in 2016

Over one-fifth of all of the points that Dan Carter scored for New Zealand were against Australia

---

Current England boss Eddie Jones managed Australia when they lost to England in the 2003 World Cup Final

---

Jonah Lomu released a video game series called 'Jonah Lomu Rugby'

---

Japan are known as the 'Brave Blossoms'

---

Wales have never reached a Rugby World Cup Final, but have finished third once, and fourth twice

Australia beat the British Isles 13-3 in their first-ever test match in 1899

England and Scotland have drawn 19 times in their history, more than any other rivalry in rugby history

The first Premiership Final to go to extra-time was in 2014, Northampton beat Saracens 24-20 after extra-time

Tim Visser and Rabz Maxwane are the only players in United Rugby Championship history to have scored 14 tries in one season, Tim Visser also managed a 13-try season the following year

In 2003, Australia scored 22 tries as they beat Namibia 142-0 in the World Cup Pools

American winger Takudzwa Ngwenya outpaced Bryan Habana in 2007, running around the outside of the Springbok sprinter to score for the Eagles from 50m out, winning World Rugby Try of the Year for his efforts

---

New Zealand and England are the only two teams to have played in four Rugby World Cup Finals

---

Toulouse won the first-ever European Rugby Champions Cup

---

Many believe that Georgia should replace Italy in the Six Nations, due to the Italian's poor form in the competition

---

Argentina have scored more points in test match history than South Africa, Ireland and Scotland

England have never lost to Italy, to date, they have played one another 29 times

---

If you kick the ball and catch it on the other side of the defensive line, this is often called a 'chip and go' or a 'chip and chase'

---

2023 will mark the 200th anniversary of when William Webb Ellis first picked up the football and ran with it at Rugby School

---

The American rugby team are known as the 'Eagles'

---

Brothers Scott, Jordie and Beauden Barrett all play for the All Blacks

The 2016–17 season saw the highest average attendance at Premiership Rugby matches in its history, with an average attendance of 15,065

---

Sir Clive Woodward managed the only England side to ever win the World Cup

---

Unsurprisingly, Dan Carter is the top point scorer in the history of the Rugby Championship

---

Chris Ashton is the only English player to have won World Rugby Try of the Year, he won it for his 2010 length-of-the-field try against the Wallabies

---

France will host the 2023 Rugby World Cup

Fiji are the most successful team in Pacific Nations Cup history, they have won five championships to Samoa's four who are runners-up

---

Loosehead props wear the number 1, tighthead props wear the number three

---

No Australian player has ever won the World Rugby Player of the Year award, despite 15 nominations

---

Scotland's Stuart Hogg is related to Manchester United legend George Best

---

As of 2022, England have won the Six Nations a record 29 times, but Wales is just one win shy, with 28 wins

England's 2003 side was the only team in history to record 16 wins in a calendar year

---

Leicester Tigers are Premiership Rugby's all-time most successful side, with 11 titles to their name

---

Warren Gatland coached the British and Irish Lions on three tours, he won one, lost one, and drew one

---

New Zealand bounced back from their 2022 loss to Argentina by beating the Pumas 53-3 in the rematch, their biggest-ever win against Argentina

---

English teams have been the most successful in Challenge Cup history, they have won 12 titles, with French sides winning 11 times

In 2022, New Zealand lost three games in a row for the first time since 1999

Richie McCaw is the only player in history to have made over 100 caps as captain of his country, he led the All Blacks out 110 times

England's Lydia Thompson received a red card in the 18th minute of the 2021 Women's Rugby World Cup Final for a high tackle

Oscar Wilde once hilariously described rugby as a "good occasion for keeping thirty bullies far from the centre of the city"

Michael Hooper became the second-ever player to reach 50 international caps before the age of 24, he won his fiftieth cap playing in the 2015 World Cup Final

Ireland defeated the All Blacks for the first time in their history in 2018, playing the match in Chicago, USA

---

The Welsh Rugby team are nicknamed 'The Dragons'

---

Chris Ashton is the Gallagher Premiership's all-time top try scorer and he is on course to become the first player to score over 100 tries in the Premiership

---

England hosted the 2015 World Cup, and it was the only time they have ever failed to qualify for the knockout stages of the tournament

---

Richard Dourthe scored over 3000 points in the Top 14, making him the competition's top point scorer of all time

New Zealand beat France 62–13 in the 2015 Rugby World Cup Quarter-Finals, the largest winning margin in the knockout stages in World Cup history

---

Ireland hooker Keith Wood won the first ever World Rugby Player of the Year award in 2001

---

Wales play their home matches at the Principality Stadium

---

Michael Hooper earnt his 50th Wallabies Cap just three years and 140 days after his debut

---

Jonah Lomu loved playing against England, he scored eight tries in seven matches against them (although four did come in one game)

Scrum-half George Gregan is the all-time most-capped player for the Wallabies, he played 139 times for Australia

---

No player has ever won the United Rugby Championship Player of the Year award twice

---

England have finished second at the World Cup three times, but never third

---

England winger Chris Ashton often does the 'Ash-Splash', where he dives over the line with the ball in one hand with both hands in the air, he hasn't dropped one...yet

---

Australia beat Scotland by one single point in the 2015 World Cup Quarter-Final following a last-minute penalty by Bernard Foley, which was awarded for a very controversial offside decision

To date, the British and Irish Lions have won 75% of their matches, lost 20% and drawn 5%

---

The Premiership Player of the Year has been won by a non-English player just three times: Martin Castrogiovanni in 2007 (Italy), Jimmy Gopperth in 2017 (New Zealand) and Vereniki Goneva in 2018 (Fiji)

---

England beat New Zealand for the first time at a Rugby World Cup in 2019, they stunned the All Blacks with a 19-7 victory in the semis

---

New Zealand are the only team that has won back-to-back World Cups, they won in 2011 and 2015

---

France won the Six Nations Grand Slam in 2022

Scotland have reached the World Cup Semi-Finals once, finishing the tournament in fourth in 1991

---

Before 1948, drop goals were worth 4 points

---

Rugby originally had 20 players on each team, but in 1877 it was decided that the number of players would be reduced to 15

---

A Japanese zoo named a giraffe after full-back Ayumu Goromaru after his amazing performances at the 2015 World Cup

---

As of the end of 2022, Australia have one won more match in Rugby Championship/Tri Nations history than South Africa

France's women won the first-ever Women's Six Nations

---

Famously the actress Elizabeth Taylor said that she preferred "rugby to soccer...I enjoy the violence in rugby, except when they start biting each other's ears off"

---

Chris Paterson is Scotland's all-time top scorer, he scored 809 in Scotland colours throughout his career

---

In rugby knockout competitions, if the score is tied at the end of extra time the match goes to a penalty shootout

---

If a tackler takes a player past the horizontal when they are making a tackle, meaning their legs come above their head, they must ensure the player is returned to the ground safely to avoid a card

New Zealand Women's team have won the World Cup a record six times, they have never lost a final

---

Fiji reached the knockout stages of the Rugby World Cup for the first time in 2007, they were beaten 37-20 by South Africa, who would go on to win the competition

---

England boss Eddie Jones once said that the winger Jack Nowell could play as a flanker

---

Jonah Lomu could run the 100m in just 11.2 seconds

---

As of 2022, there have been 1207 players to play for the All Blacks in their history

Ben Smith is the only player to ever receive a yellow card in a Rugby World Cup Final

---

Jonny Wilkinson scored more drop goals in international rugby than any other player in history, with his 36 successful drop kicks for England

---

The Ireland Rugby team includes players from both the Republic of Ireland and Northern Ireland

---

The Junior All Blacks won all 13 of the matches they played in the Pacific Nations Cup

---

England's Josh Lewsey scored after 79 seconds of the 2007 Rugby World Cup Semi-Final against France, it was the fastest try in the history of the knockout stages of the Rugby World Cup

No scrum-half has ever won the Premiership Player of the Year award

In 2001, England beat Italy 80-23, in the highest-scoring match in Six Nations history

The sin bin was introduced to rugby in 2001, it had been used in Rugby League since 1981

The most tries Dan Carter scored against any nation was Wales, in just nine matches he scored five tries

Julian Savea scored 46 tries in just 54 caps for the All Blacks

England's women have scored 80 points or more five times in Six Nations matches, no other side has achieved this feat once

---

Serge Blanco is France's all-time top try scorer, he scored 38 tries between 1980 and 1991

---

Former Sale and Saracens fly-half Charlie Hodgson is the Gallagher Premiership's all-time top point scorer, he scored 2625 points in 16 years in the Premiership

---

England Rugby won 90% of their games from 2000-2003

---

Both the final and third place play-off in the 2007 Rugby World Cup were replays of matches that had occurred in the group stages, this had never once happened before in the history of the Rugby World Cup

Rugby was introduced to South Africa by the British troops who were stationed in Cape Town

---

Until the 2024-25 season, Premiership Rugby teams have a combined salary cap of £5 million per year

---

Wallabies Full Back Israel Folau played professionally in Rugby Union, Rugby League and Australian Rules Football

---

Toulon, London Wasps, Bath and Exeter Chiefs are the only teams to have a 100% winning record in the European Rugby Champions Cup Final

---

Props are typically the heaviest players on a rugby team

England's women won the Six Nations Grand Slam in 2022

New Zealand is the only team that South Africa does not have a winning record against

When Wales faced France in the semi-final of the 2011 World Cup, Welsh captain Sam Warburton was sent off for a dangerous tackle just 19 minutes into the game, Wales still lost by just one point

Many regard the Jonah Lomu Rugby video game series as the best series of rugby games ever produced

Henry Arundell won the 2021-22 Premiership Rugby Young Player of the Year award

South Africa's Bryan Habana has scored the most tries for a player in a Tier 1 nation in rugby history

---

Former All Black fly-half Stephen Donald is nicknamed 'The Beaver', his local rugby club renamed their home ground to Beaver Park after he won the World Cup

---

Pakistan's rugby team is nicknamed the 'The Greenshirts'

---

Samoa's pre-match performance is not called the Haka, instead, it is known as the 'Siva Tau'

---

In 2021, Italy conceded a record 239 points in the Six Nations

The European Rugby Champions Cup was known as the Heineken Cup until 2014 when it had a rebrand

---

Scotland's best-ever IRB World Ranking was fifth, they reached this in 2017 and 2018

---

Australia's heaviest World Cup defeat came against England in 2019, they lost 40-16 in the quarter-finals, this was also the match in which they conceded the most points

---

Replacement fly-half Freddie Burns scored a drop-goal in the 79th minute to win the Gallagher Premiership 15-12 for Leicester in 2022

---

If a player kicks the ball straight into touch, without it bouncing before, and they are outside of their 22, the ball is called 'out on the full', and the lineout takes place from where the kick was taken

France have reached the World Cup Final three times and have never lifted the trophy

Argentina finally beat New Zealand for the first time in 2020, they beat them again in 2022

Freddie Stewart scored his first try for England against Australia

The British and Irish Lions have beaten the All Blacks six times but have lost 29 times

England won the first edition of the Six Nations, known then as the 'Home Nations', in 1883

Dan Carter is the top scorer in Crusaders history, he scored 1708 points for his club

---

Clermont and Racing 92 have both reached the final of the European Rugby Champions Cup three times without ever winning the competition

---

Ten South Africa-born players have played for Scotland in recent years, most notably perhaps is winger Duhan van der Merwe

---

Wales' 1905 match against New Zealand saw Wales defeat the All Blacks in what was called 'The Game of the Century'

---

Australia lost to Italy for the first time in 2022, they lost 28-27 to the Italians

Wales, England, Scotland and Ireland all compete for the Triple Crown trophy in the Six Nations

New Zealand and South Africa both won four and lost two matches in the 2022 Rugby Championship, New Zealand earned one more bonus point which helped them win the competition

Brian O'Driscoll is the only player to have ever won the Six Nations Championship Player of the Championship three times

Australia's 40-14 loss in 2022 to New Zealand dropped them to ninth in the World Rankings, their lowest-ever position

French and English teams have won a record ten European Rugby Champions Cups each

The Barbarians have a great record against Ireland, they have won five and lost just once against the Irish

---

South Africa didn't compete in the 2020 Rugby Championship, due to the Covid-19 pandemic, and so the tournament was held as a 'Tri-Nations Series' with just New Zealand, Australia and Argentina

---

Beauden Barrett has scored the most Super Rugby points of any active player, he got passed to 1300-point mark in 2022

---

Australia have a winning record against every Northern Hemisphere team aside from England

---

England's women have won the Six Nations a record 18 times, 12 more than France in second place

There are over 180,000 registered rugby clubs worldwide

---

The Rugby World Cup trophy is named after William Webb Ellis, who is often credited with inventing rugby

---

Former All Black centre Sonny Bill Williams began his career playing Rugby League, then won the World Cup in Rugby Union before becoming the World Boxing Association International Heavyweight Champion

---

The new 50:22 rule means that if a player kicks the ball from their own half, and it goes out inside the opponent's 22 after bouncing in field, the team that kicked the ball gets to throw in the lineout

---

Australia was the first team in history to win two Rugby World Cups, they won in 1991 and 1999, but have not won since

Bath, Leicester and Gloucester are the only three teams that have played in every season of Premiership Rugby

---

Tonga's war dance that they perform pre-match is called the 'Sipi Tau'

---

Chile will be the only team to make their debut at the 2023 Rugby World Cup

---

If a team is said to attack down the 'blindside' this is referring to the narrower side of the pitch from where the breakdown or scrum was, often this area has fewer defenders and can catch the defending team off guard

---

No Welsh side has ever won the European Rugby Champions Cup

South Africa's 2022 26-10 win over the All Blacks saw them win by the biggest margin against the All Blacks since 1928

---

New Zealand were the seventh team to make their international debut, they played for the first time in 1903

---

There were no tries scored in the 2007 World Cup Final, where South Africa won 15-6 v. England

---

England's women lost by just 3 points to the Black Ferns in the 2021 World Cup Final, despite playing for an hour with 14 players

---

Rugby balls switched from pigs bladders to rubber tubing as the bladders were causing those who had to blow them up to fall ill, due to diseases carried in the bladders

Richmond Women and Saracens Women both won a record five titles in the Women's Premiership before it was discontinued in 2017

---

Welsh refereeing legend Nigel Owens has refereed a record seven European Rugby Champions Cup Finals

---

England's victory over New Zealand in 2019 was the first time New Zealand didn't score a point in the first half of a Rugby World Cup match since 1991

---

In New Zealand, the changing rooms are known as the 'sheds'

---

Jonny Wilkinson scored eight drop goals at the 2003 World Cup

Connacht John Muldoon played 254 times in the United Rugby Championship, more than any other player

Ireland's heaviest World Cup defeat came in the 2019 quarter-finals against New Zealand, they lost 46-14

Aussie full-back Israel Folau is Super Rugby's all-time top try scorer, with 60 tries for the Waratahs in just six years with the club

The British and Irish Lions have won the majority of their matches against Australia, with 17 wins and 6 losses to the Wallabies to date

Martin Johnson was the England captain when they won the World Cup

New Zealand didn't score a point in the second half of their 20-16 win against Argentina in 2019, the first time they failed to register in the second half in this fixture's history

---

Maro Itoje, Owen Farrell and David Pocock have all received three nominations for World Rugby Player of the Year, without ever winning the award

---

Jonah Lomu scored seven tries in six games against Scotland

---

Despite kicking off in the early afternoon, the New Zealand v Scotland tie in 1978 was played in the dark, due to Scotland's winter conditions and the fact there were no floodlights in Murrayfield at the time

---

Dan Carter had a 100% winning record against all but four of his international opponents, the worst record he had was against Australia, who he still had a 74% winning record against

No player has ever won European Rugby Champions Cup Player of the Year twice

---

Wallaby Peter FitzSimons once hilariously describes the difference between backs and forwards in rugby, suggesting "Rugby backs can be identified because they generally have clean jerseys and identifiable partings in their hair"

---

Harlequins play their home games at 'The Stoop'

---

In a rugby penalty shootout, five kicks are taken by each team, if the scores are tied after five kicks each then sudden death is called

---

Andrea Masi is the only Italian player to have ever won the Six Nations Championship Player of the Championship

England's women won 30 matches in a row, becoming the first team to ever achieve this when they beat Canada in the 2021 Rugby World Cup Semi-Final

---

Damian Penaud became the first French player to win World Rugby Try of the Year in 2021

---

Sam Warburton was the 800th player to play for the British and Irish Lions, and he went on to captain them for two tours

---

The Super 14 Final of 2006 between the Crusaders and the Hurricanes was covered in such a thick layer of mist, that you could not see from one side of the pitch to the other, the Crusaders won a cagey 16-9

---

Wales won their first ever Six Nations (or Home Nations as it was known at the time) in 1908

Munster legend Ronan O'Gara has made the most appearances in the European Rugby Champions Cup, with 110 appearances in the competition

---

A 'choke tackle' is when the defender tries to hold onto their opponent and keep them on their feet, typically this leads to a scrum for the defending team if executed correctly

---

Argentina have won at least one test match against every Tier 1 nation

---

In 1939, a match between New Zealand sides Southland and Manawatu was played on a pitch covered in snow, parts of the pitch were covered in ten inches

---

Richard Wigglesworth is the only player to have played over 300 matches in the Gallagher Premiership, playing for Sale, Saracens and Leicester in his over 20-year-long career

The Crusaders never lost to Argentine club side Jaguares, they have a 100% winning record

---

Former England winger Christian Wade spent three seasons playing for the NFL side Buffalo Bills' practice squad but was unable to break into their first team

---

Owen Farrell celebrates every successful kick he scores by linking his fingers together to make a 'JJ' sign, the 'Joining Jack' symbol, which represents a charity that help sufferers of Duchenne muscular dystrophy

---

Protesters dropped 'flour bombs' on the New Zealand v South Africa match from low-flying planes in 1981 as well as flares, New Zealand won the match despite the distractions 25-22

---

Doug Howlett is the All Black's top try scorer of all time, he dotted down 49 times for New Zealand

You are not allowed to touch another player whilst they are in the air

---

Australia and New Zealand have drawn eight times

---

Tommy Bowe scored a record 67 tries in the United Rugby Championship

---

England World Cup winner Jason Robinson began his career playing rugby league, before moving over to playing union

---

There are 6.6 million registered rugby players in the world

In 2020, 20 players representing Scotland were foreign-born, five from South Africa, six English, three Australian, five New Zealanders and one Spanish player

Saracens were relegated from the Premiership in 2020 after they broke salary cap rules, they were promoted back into the Premiership the following season

Player GPS has identified Christian Wade as the fastest player in rugby history, he achieved a top speed of 11.2 metres per second

Coventry, Liverpool St Helens, Moseley, Nottingham, Rosslyn Park, Waterloo and Rugby only appeared in the Premiership during the amateur era, Exeter Chiefs, Leeds, London Welsh, Richmond, Worcester and Rotherham have only played Premiership Rugby in the professional era

Whilst Scotland have never beaten the All Blacks, they have beaten South Africa five times and the Wallabies on twelve occasions

Fiji's pre-match ritual dance is known as the 'Cibi'

---

If you catch a kick inside your own 22, you can call a 'mark', which allows you to clear the ball without pressure from the opposition

---

A try was scored in the 76th and 78th minute of the 2021 Premiership Rugby Final, first by Harlequins and then by Exeter, Harlequins edged the tie by winning 40-38

---

No Scottish side has ever won the European Rugby Champions Cup

---

Sonny Bill Williams is the most followed rugby player on Instagram, with over 1 million followers

Blindside flankers wear the number 6, openside flankers wear the number 7

---

The Blues topped the Super Rugby table in 2022 but were defeated in the Super Rugby Final

---

An up-and-under kick, where the ball is kicked high with the intention of competing for the ball in the air, is sometimes referred to as a 'Garryowen'

---

The first rugby penalty shootout was played between Leicester Tigers and Cardiff Blues in the semi-final of the 2009 Heineken Cup, Leicester won 7-6

---

New Zealand have hosted two of the three World Cup tournaments that they have won

Not only is Chris Ashton Premiership Rugby's top try scorer, he also has the most tries in the European Rugby Champions Cup, and is the only player with over 40 tries in the competition

---

Former England winger Mark Cueto didn't play rugby until he was 17 and made his professional debut at 22

---

A young George North once iconically lifted Israel Folau over his shoulder and charged forward, when Folau was supposed to be tackling North

---

Owen Farrell's father is the head coach of Ireland

---

Until 1884, most teams played with nine forwards, and just five backs, this all changed as Cardiff wanted their pacey back Frank Hancock to get on the pitch, but didn't want to remove any player from their back-line, so changed their formation and it has stuck ever since

England and Harlequins fly-half Marcus Smith was born in Manila, Philippines

---

Sergio Parisse is Italy's most-capped international ever, with 142 caps for Italy, only Alun Wyn Jones and Richie McCaw have more international caps

---

Beauden Barrett is the only fly-half to have scored over 40 tries for the All Blacks

---

Rugby is the national sport of Georgia, Tonga and Madagascar

---

Jonah Lomu scored five tries in just three matches against Italy

Jonny Wilkinson is the only rugby player to ever win the BBC Sports Personality of the Year

The so-called "try from the end of the world" was scored in a match between France and New Zealand in 1994, involving 10 France players in a blistering counter-attack, it is known as one of the best tries ever

Wales were ranked as the world's top side according to the IRB World Rankings in 2019, just six years earlier they were tenth

In New Zealand, the fly-half position is often referred to as a 'first five-eighth'

Jack Anderton is recorded as the first ever British and Irish Lion, he was capped in 1888 as part of the first test tour for the Lions

Dan Parks scored a record 1582 points in the United Rugby Championship

---

Switching direction with a step following a hop in the air is often called a 'Goose Step', Marcus Smith and Quade Cooper are two of rugby's finest goose steppers

---

Before it was known as the Gallagher Premiership, it was called the Aviva Premiership, and even before that it was the Guinness Premiership

---

Dan Carter is the most followed rugby player on Facebook

---

Shane Williams is the only Welsh player to ever win World Rugby Player of the Year, he won his award in 2008

Nicknamed 'The Waterpolo Test', New Zealand beat Scotland 24-0 in 1975 on a pitch covered with so much rain, some were fearful that players may even drown if they were in a ruck in some parts of the pitch

---

French teams have finished as European Rugby Champions Cup runners-up a record 16 times

---

Western Samoa shocked the world in 1991, beating Wales 16-13 in the World Cup

---

Munster's Ben Healy missed both of his penalties in a penalty shoot-out against Toulouse in 2022, Toulouse won 4-2

---

Most coaches call the area between the try line and the 22-metre line the 'red zone'

Printed in Great Britain
by Amazon

29347347R00056